MOUNTAINBIKE!
SOUTHWEST WASHINGTON

A GUIDE TO TRAILS & ADVENTURE

MOUNTAINBIKE!
SOUTHWEST WASHINGTON

A GUIDE TO TRAILS & ADVENTURE

JOHNZILLY

SASQUATCH BOOKS
SEATTLE

Acknowledgments

To everyone who helped me on this book with encouraging words, inspiring ideas, critiques, food, trail suggestions, love, and patience at my guidebook-writing ways—thank you so much. It is not hyperbole to say that I would not have completed this book without all of your help, right down to the last Jolly Rancher offered and accepted 23 miles into an epic. I'd especially like to thank Steve DeBroux for his research help and all those excellent stories, and Angela Castañeda for her love and support.

Printed in the United States of America.
Distributed in Canada by Raincoast Books Ltd.
02 01   5 4 3 2

Cover and interior design and composition: Kate Basart
Cover photograph: ©1998 Steve Bonni/Graphistock
Research assistance: Steve DeBroux
Interior photographs: John Zilly, Wade Praeger, Steve DeBroux, Greg Strong, Lisa Strong, David Graves, Paul Smale, Danny McMillin

Library of Congress Cataloging in Publication Data
Zilly, John.
    Mountain bike! southwest Washington : a guide to trails and adventure
/ John Zilly.
         p.   cm.
       ISBN 1-57061-137-8
       1. All terrain cycling—Washington (State)—Guidebooks. 2. Bicycle trails—
    Washington (State)—Guidebooks. 3. Washington (State)—Guidebooks. I. Title.
GV1045.5.W2Z45 1998
917.97'80443—dc21   98-2668

SASQUATCH BOOKS
615 Second Avenue
Seattle, Washington 98104
(206) 467-4300
books@sasquatchbooks.com
http://www.sasquatchbooks.com

Sasquatch Books publishes high-quality adult nonfiction and children's books related to the Northwest (Alaska to San Francisco). For more information about our titles, contact us at the address above, or view our site on the World Wide Web.

Southwest Washington

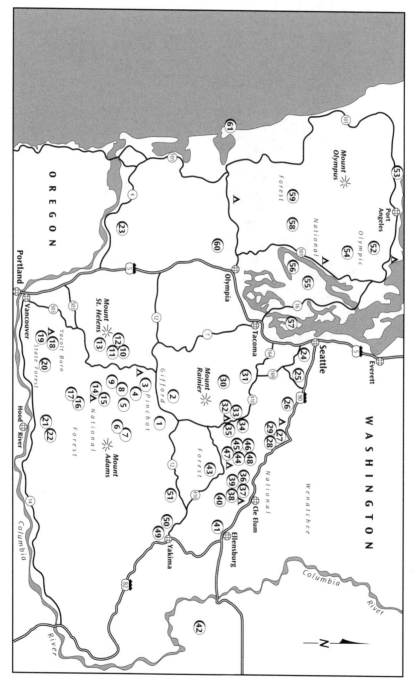

Contents

Rides by Difficulty, Season, Views

EASY ✷

Ride №	Ride Name	Spring	Summer	Fall	Winter	Views
26	Boxley Creek	●	●	●	●	
28	Keechelus Lake	◐	●	●		●
61	Ocean Shores	●	●	●	●	●

INTERMEDIATE ✷✷

Ride №	Ride Name	Spring	Summer	Fall	Winter	Views
1	Packwood Lake	◐	●	●		●
7	Horseshoe Lake		●	●		●
16	Lone Butte		●	●		●
27	Snoqualmie Tunnel		●			
30	Carbon River Road	◐	●	●		
42	Crab Creek	●		●	●	
50	Cowiche Ridgeline	●	●	●		
51	Tieton River	●	●	●		
53	Spruce Railroad Trail	●	●	●	●	●

DIFFICULT ✷✷✷

Ride №	Ride Name	Spring	Summer	Fall	Winter	Views
2	Skate Creek	◐	●	●		●
3	Kraus Ridge		●	●		
4	Tongue Mountain		●	●		
6	High Lakes		●	●		●
8	Three Buttes		●	●		●
10	Norway Pass		●	●		●
12	Plains of Abraham		●	●		●
17	Oldman Pass		●	●		
20	Three Corner Rock	◐	●	●		
21	Nestor Peak	◐	●	●		●
22	Buck Creek	◐	●	●		
23	Elochoman State Forest	●	●	●	●	
24	Tapeworm Trail	●	●	●	●	
29	Mount Catherine		●	●		●
31	Mud Mountain Rim Trail	●	●	●	●	
37	North Fork Taneum Creek	●	●	●		

38	Fishhook Flats	●	●	●		
40	South Fork Manastash Creek		●	●		
41	Manastash Ridge	●	●	●		●
46	West Fork Bear Creek	◑	●	●		
47	Quartz Creek		●	●		
49	Cowiche Canyon	●	●	●		
54	Lower Big Quilcene		●	●		
55	Beaver Pond Trail	●	●	●	●	●
56	Twin Lakes Trail	●	●	●	●	
57	Section 31	●	●	●	●	
58	South Fork Skokomish River	●	●	●		

MORE DIFFICULT ✦✦✦✦

Ride №	Ride Name	Spring	Summer	Fall	Winter	Views
7	Badger Ridge		●	●		●
13	Ape Canyon		●	●		●
14	Lewis River		●	●		
15	Cussed Hollow		●	●		
18	Tarbell Trail	◑	●	●		
19	Larch Mountain	◑	●	●		●
25	Preston Railroad Trail	●	●	●		
32	Sun Top		●	◑		●
33	Skookum Flats		●			
34	Ranger Creek		●	●		●
35	Crystal Mountain		●	◑		●
39	Taneum Ridge	◑	●	●		
43	Little Bald Mountain		●	●		●
44	Crow Creek		●	●		
45	Raven Roost		●	◑		
48	Mount Clifty		●	●		●
52	Dungeness River		●	●		
59	Wynoochee Lake		●	●		
60	Fall Creek	●	●	●	●	

EXTREME EPIC ✦✦✦✦✦

Ride №	Ride Name	Spring	Summer	Fall	Winter	Views
5	Juniper Ridge Epic		◑	●		●
11	Smith Creek Epic		●	●		●
36	Lookout Mountain Epic		●	●		●

About the Author

John Zilly is the Northwest's very own mountain biking guru. In 1980, fresh out of high school, he spent nine months circumnavigating the United States by bike, surviving 57 flats and pedaling more than 10,500 miles. After also touring Europe from the saddle, he exchanged his thin tires for fat ones and has been exploring the dirt trails of the Northwest ever since. He is the author of six mountain biking guidebooks, including the best-selling *Kissing the Trail*, a guide to rides near Seattle, and *Mountain Bike! Northwest Washington*, the companion to this volume. John researches all the routes himself and creates his maps using GPS tracking data. John lives in Seattle with his wife, Angela.

Trail On!

Perhaps my first mistake was buying those shiny green tire levers. Not that there weren't other mistakes, of course, but when I think back on it, I remember seeing those green tire levers on the display rack. And that was the beginning of the trouble, though Baldy didn't see it that way.

I had gone to the store for a couple of inner tubes, nothing else. I already had tire levers that worked fine, but those new tire levers caught my eye. A week later, on a hot August evening near the Little Naches River, I was 13 miles into a 20-mile ride-all singletrack. It had been a good day. My T-shirt was soaked from the strenuous climb, my arms dusty from the hike-a-biking. The sun had recently disappeared over the last ridge of the day, but the sky still glowed in orange and blue light. Only the perfect 6-mile descent remained, and I looked forward to it.

I corkscrewed down the ridgeline, smile wide, calories ebbing. If all went according to the master plan, in 30 minutes I'd be back at the trailhead where Baldy, who had decided to fish all day, would be cleaning "some big fatties" for dinner. I zipped around a few more corners, gained a little speed, then bunny-hopped a series of roots. But I came down hard on my rear tire, and 20 yards down the trail it was flat. I nodded. I'd lost myself in the moment. That's okay, I said to myself, I'd have the flat fixed in 5 minutes and be back on the trail. The 6-mile descent still to come.

This, however, is when the master plan cracked and was demoted to simply the plan, soon to be failed. The new green tire levers didn't work. After 45 minutes of wrestling with my tire, it was still flat and affixed to the rim. The combination of a tight tire and rubbery tire levers proved unworkable. Regret—at actually spending money for these useless pieces of plastic and then carrying them all day—was making a strong move down the backstretch. My future was suddenly clear. In twilight, I began riding toward the trailhead on a flat rear tire, the wobbly back end fishtailing around dusty corners, the rim clanking on loose rocks. Gone was the epic descent, gone was the fun, gone was the light and my smile-creased face.

When I arrived at the trailhead—swearing up a storm—Baldy was still fishing, casting into the dark river with the help of a headlamp. I explained what had happened—the flat, the tire levers, the last 6 miles. The punch line was supposed to be about how I'd missed the perfect downhill because of the evil green tire levers, how I'd been charmed, waylaid, then humiliated by the tire lever genies. He grinned and with his usual effusiveness said, "You just rode that blazing 6-mile descent on a flat tire? That is so cool. Trail on!"

Whoa! Isn't this where I get to bitterly complain about my unfortunate lot?

"Now let's get to camp so we can cook up the big fatties I caught this afternoon."

Back at camp I remembered those last 6 flat-tire miles. It had been interesting, for sure. I remembered the abrupt, choppy roll and swell of the trail as the light dimmed and the air cooled. I fishtailed and balanced, and around the corners I relied on a lot more finesse than zip. As I stared into the camp fire and ate the fresh trout, my smile returned.

Choosing a Ride

You ought to be able to easily and efficiently select a ride, get to the trailhead, and then negotiate the route (for epic rides, all bets are off). That should be the guiding principle, so to speak. It's my hope that *Mountain Bike! Southwest Washington* functions that way for you. The following describes the rating system, explains how the information is presented, and provides an annotated look at some of the wording conventions I use to detail each ride.

Difficulty Rating

The difficulty rating is measured in wheels, ranging from one to five, with one wheel being easiest and five wheels being hardest. The difficulty rating is based on the length of the trip, the hill factor and elevation gain, and the level of bike-handling skill required. This quick reference is located near the title of each ride.

⚙ *(easy):* Just about anyone can accomplish a ride rated as one wheel; it isn't much different from riding on a paved country road. These rides are short and flat, and have well-packed riding surfaces. One-wheel rides stick to wide, smooth dirt roads or rail-trails.

⚙⚙ *(intermediate):* Two-wheel rides primarily traverse dirt roads and rail-trails, although they occasionally venture onto easily negotiated doubletrack and singletrack for short stretches. These rides are somewhat longer and may have more elevation gain than those rated one wheel. These routes never demand a high skill level, and riders will rarely hike-a-bike.

⚙⚙⚙ *(difficult):* More rides in this book receive this rating than any other. These routes—all of which contain some singletrack—travel less than 20 miles and have moderate elevation gains, generally less than 1,600 feet. Typically, a ride rated three wheels combines a dirt-road climb with a singletrack descent. Be prepared for at least a few steep climbs as well as some technical sections of trail that may require hike-a-biking.

⚙⚙⚙⚙ *(most difficult):* If a ride is long, hilly, and chock-full of challenging singletrack, I have rated it four wheels. Some riders may have to push or carry their bikes for long distances. You'll gain big chunks of elevation and have your bike-handling skills tested on every four wheeler. Remember: If you're not hiking, you're not mountain biking.

⚙⚙⚙⚙⚙ *(extreme epic):* Three rides in this book are sufficiently difficult to warrant an extreme, epic rating of five wheels. These rides are very long, technical, hilly, and, at times, dangerous, usually requiring miles of walking or hike-a-biking as well as complex route-finding. Do not attempt them unless you are an expert mountain bicyclist, in great physical condition, and enjoy pushing yourself to the limit.

Ride Statistics

Distance
This information is given in miles.

Ride
I have noted the format of each route here, either Loop or Out & Back, as well as the types of trails and roads the route traverses. On some rides, the word **views** appears on this line. Of course every ride has *some* view, but if a ride is marked as a views ride, then on clear days you should expect to see a snow-capped volcano, a spectacular mountain lake, a panoramic vista, or all of the above.

Duration
The duration of a ride depends on your skill, stamina, and map-reading abilities, as well as what you did the previous night. Trail conditions and weather can also drastically alter the time it takes to complete a ride. Before you leave, call to find out about current trail and weather conditions.

Travel time
Estimated driving times are listed, usually from the nearest two major cities.

Hill factor
"How hard are the hills?" is often the first question cyclists ask about a given route. This quick reference describes the difficulty of the climbs. The elevation gain, measured from the ride's low point to high point, is also listed. (By the way, singletrack climbs that average more than 300 feet per mile and road climbs that average more than 450 feet per mile are very difficult.)

Skill level
Rides are rated for beginner, intermediate, advanced, or expert, depending on the minimum bike-handling ability a rider should have before attempting a particular trail. This rating has nothing to do with fitness; you may be a fine athlete, but I wouldn't recommend an expert trail if you have never mountain biked before.

Season
This entry lists the best time of year to be out on this trail. Seasonal trail closures are also noted. Call the managing agency for current trail conditions and restrictions.

Maps
Supplementary maps are key, unless you enjoy bivouacking. I typically recommend United States Geological Survey (USGS) topographical maps, United States Forest Service district maps, Green Trails maps, or Washington State Forest maps.

Users
This entry notes what types of users are likely to be out on the trail.

More info
Here the agency that manages each trail is named, and its phone number is provided. For current trail conditions, maintenance schedule, snow level, permit information, and other restrictions, call ahead.

Prelude

Each ride begins with a descriptive overview, which paints a landscape and recounts trail anecdotes.

To Get There

This paragraph provides detailed instructions for driving to the trailhead. In most cases, I have indicated a point at which you should set the trip odometer in your car to zero.

The Ride

In addition to notes about the terrain and landscape, and an occasional quip, the ride section contains a detailed description of the route—up or down, left or right. These paragraphs note the mileage—in bold—for most intersections, hills, tricky sections of trail, vistas, and other significant landmarks. Riding with an odometer is highly recommended.

What follows is an annotated listing of some of the conventions I use in describing the trails in *Mountain Bike! Southwest Washington*. WHOA! signifies a dangerous section of trail or a turn easily missed, and warns the rider to pay close attention. **Stay on the main trail/road** means that other trails or roads exit from the main trail—use good judgment to continue on the primary trail or road. When the trail dead-ends at another trail, forcing a 90-degree turn either right or left, the resulting three-way intersection is described as a **T**. Other three-way intersections are usually described as **forks**, though sometimes I write that the **trail divides**. If a faint trail **(lesser trail)** forks off the main trail, I will sometimes tell you to **ignore** it or **pass** it rather than describe it as a fork. When two trails or roads cross, the result is usually referred to as a **four-way intersection**. On many trails you'll have to **walk** or **push** your bike up a steep hill. If, however, a long stretch of trail requires an awkward combination of walking and riding, I describe it as a **hike-a-bike**. A **technical** section of trail—typically a narrow tread or steep slope populated by roots, rocks, or other obstacles—demands good bike-handling skills. On unmaintained trails or on trails transformed by clearcutting and road building, it's sometimes difficult to figure out which way to go. In these instances, I'll probably mention the problematic **route-finding**.

There are a number of different types of trails and roads described in this book. A dirt or gravel **road** could be used by a car. Roads in national forests are usually identified by a number preceded by **FR** for Forest Road. **Doubletracks**, also know as **jeep trails**, **jeep tracks**, or **old roads**, refer to narrow, rough roads and may be either motorized or nonmotorized. Often, these old roads are **gated** to keep out motor vehicles. Old railroad grades, or **rail-trails**, are abandoned railroad lines that have no tracks or ties. Typically, rail-trails have the look and feel of dirt roads, except that rail-trails are usually flat and nonmotorized. **Trail** and **singletrack**, terms that are used interchangeably, generally refer to soft-surface trails less than 36 inches wide. A **wide trail** refers to a path 3 to 8 feet wide. Sometimes, however, "trail" is used in a generic sense to mean any part of a route, whether paved or soft-surface, between 12 inches and 12 feet wide.

Option

For some rides, I have provided directions to modify the route. Occasionally the option shortens the trip, but in most cases it adds mileage and difficulty, often to bag a peak or catch a nice view.

Gazetteer

Each ride concludes with information on nearby campgrounds and services. The information on the nearest town helps pinpoint the ride's location, or at least lets you know which direction to head to satisfy that Iced Animal Cookie craving. Use the information noted under the Gazetteer heading to plan weekend trips. Often several rides start from the same trailhead or can be accessed from the same campground.

The Maps and GPS Features

I recorded the route, mileage, and elevation data using a Global Positioning System (GPS) receiver, a cycle computer, and an altimeter. Using these tools, I created maps for *Mountain Bike! Southwest Washington* that have a lot of cool features.

The most unique feature of the maps is certainly the GPS data. Using a network of space-based satellites, GPS receivers monitor and track latitude and longitude. I recorded the twists and turns of every route, then used that track data to create the maps. In some cases, the maps in *Mountain Bike!* are more accurate than any existing map. (Keep in mind, though, that recreational GPS receivers have a small error factor.) In addition to recording the track data, I used the receiver to make a series of waypoints (GPS lingo for an exact location) for each ride, which I call Ridepoints. Individual Ridepoints are marked by numbered triangles at key junctures along the ride; you'll also find a complete list of Ridepoints—a route—for each ride in a small box on the map.

The Ridepoint numbers are latitude and longitude coordinates (WGS 84 map datum). Ridepoint 1 is the trailhead. To use the Ridepoints, punch the coordinates into your GPS receiver the night before a ride. The following day, your receiver will point toward each successive Ridepoint for the entire loop.

Additional map features: The start and finish of each ride is clearly visible, and the highlighted route prevents map face—squinted eyes and a furrowed brow. Arrows indicate the direction of travel, and mileages are noted between the triangular Ridepoints. The small graphs tell the basic elevation story of each ride, and key elevations are noted along the route.

Safety: Keep the Rubber Side Down

At the top of a particularly long, ear-popping descent, a friend turned to me and said, "Have fun and keep the rubber side down." He smiled, and pedaled away. The smile on his face indicated he was having fun. As for his second piece of advice, well, let's just say he didn't heed it. For historical accuracy: When we finished the downhill he didn't say, "You've got to try that skin-side-down technique sometime." Humorous, except for the fact that losing skin is perhaps one of the least painful scenarios.

Though it's probably more dangerous to drive to the trailhead, bicycling injuries such as cracked collarbones, dislocated shoulders, fractured wrists, and broken heads are all too common. True, no matter how much care you take, the occasional header is inevitable. If lucky, you'll be able to hop up and shake it off, but if you've sustained serious injuries, extra clothes and a first-aid kit can save your life.

Of course, the danger of mountain biking isn't just the spectacular crash. A simple mechanical failure, a sore knee, a wrong turn, or exhaustion can strand you miles from the trailhead and force an unplanned night in the woods. If you don't have the proper supplies and a friend to plan strategy with, you could be in trouble. Ironically, the worst trouble is often self-inflicted: It originates out of panic and hysteria. If you can stay calm, if you have enough to eat and drink, and if you have an extra layer of clothing to put on, you will probably be fine no matter how dire the situation seems.

Before You Leave

How's the trail? Is it hunting season? Call the managing agency.

Call the National Weather Service, 206-526-6087.

Let someone know where you plan to ride.

During the Ride

- Never ride alone.
- Always wear a helmet.
- Wear eye protection.
- Avoid excessive speed. Ride as if a small child is around every corner.
- Carry a first-aid kit.
- Carry extra clothes and a hat, no matter how nice the weather seems.
- Pack sunscreen, a lighter, a pocket knife, extra food, and a flashlight.
- Drink at least two quarts of water per day. Don't count on finding water.
- Carry a map of the area and bring a compass.
- Use a cycle computer.

Recommended Tools

- pump
- patch kit
- extra tube
- tire irons
- spoke wrench
- chain tool
- Allen wrenches
- needle-nose pliers
- crescent wrench
- screwdriver
- spare brake cable

Live on Earth: The Trail-Use Debate

I recently had an eye-opening conversation with a local Sierra Club leader about the Middle Fork of the Snoqualmie River Trail near North Bend, Washington. The Middle Fork Trail—beautiful and wild, through old growth along the river—was the only singletrack in the North Bend Ranger District that was open to bicycles. The rangers there had been managing the trail as open to bicycles since it was rebuilt (using multi-use money, by the way) in 1992. However, after several years of pestering, the Sierra Club managed to goad the Forest Service into closing the Middle Fork Trail to bikes. I asked this Sierra Clubber why they had done that, why it had been necessary to close the last trail in the district to bikes, especially when bicyclists were the primary users. He said that since the trail hadn't been hardened with concrete pavers, it wasn't appropriate for bikes. Hikers, he said, didn't want to walk through any mud on their winter outings along the Middle Fork.

Clearly, he didn't know the first thing about bicycles or trails. No one advocates building nonmotorized trails with concrete pavers. And the newest scientific studies (*Erosional Impact of Hikers, Horses, Motorcycles, and Off-Road Bicycles on Mountain Trails in Montana*, Wilson and Seney, 1994) show that hikers and mountain bikers have about the same erosional effect on trails, even in wet conditions. So his boots are going to get muddy even without bikes on the trail.

But I'm not out to get into a who-does-more-damage argument, or even blast the Sierra Club. I'm a member myself, and I believe in much of what we have accomplished over the years. In fact, more than 65 percent of mountain bicyclists consider themselves environmentalists. Call me radical, but with hundreds of trails open for hiking in the North Bend Ranger District, it seems unreasonable to close the last section of singletrack open to bicycles because some guy doesn't like to get mud on his boots when he goes hiking in February. That's not "environmental," that's selfish recreational elitism. The local Sierra Club chapter should work on improving the environment rather than alienating a big group of environmentalists over a short section of trail.

The real issue behind recreational elitism is often overcrowding. Indeed, some trails are overcrowded, but if you are willing to drive a little farther to the trailhead, you'll find that many trails aren't overcrowded, even on August weekends. This area is growing fast, and all recreationalists—even hikers—need to tailor their expectations. If you do choose to use a trail that's convenient and popular, then it's absurd to have great expectations of a solitary meditation out on the trail. And if you want to hike in February on a soft-surface trail in western Washington, plan to get your boots dirty.

Our Responsibility

Like all trail users, we need to take responsibility for the way we behave out on the trails. If we adversely affect the environment or frighten other trail users, then we shouldn't be there. Out-of-control speed freaks who skid down the trail or scare other users have no rights to the trail.

Most bicyclists, however, search out the magic that's hidden around each bend in the trail—the mossy old growth, the spawning salmon. We can't deny that mountain biking is great fun. And why should we? Being out in nature should be a joyous, not solemn, occasion. Just remember that you can be joyous without abusing the trail or the other users on it.

Cyclists have been a central part of the conservation movement for years—commuting, vacationing, and doing errands on bicycles. Bicyclists have been building and sharing soft-surface trails in western Washington for more than 100 years. In fact, bicyclists helped invent the idea of wilderness recreation. For that good tradition to continue, we need to keep searching for that magic, yielding the path to others, riding gently, and helping to maintain trails. Also, be aware that state and federal user fees are coming. Many national forests already require a permit to park at trailheads.

The Rules

- Don't leave any trace.
- Don't skid—ever. Take it easy on poorly constructed trails, and avoid wet trails or trails liable to be marred by tires. Walk around all delicate areas.
- Respect all other trail users. Yield the right of way to everyone, including hikers, runners, other bicyclists, motorcyclists, and equestrians.
- Stop and dismount when you encounter horses. Stand on the downhill side of the trail, and talk to the horse and rider as they pass.
- Always ride in control.
- Respect wildlife (you are in their home!) and livestock.

The Land You Are On

Most of the rides in *Mountain Bike! Southwest Washington* traverse trails and roads on public land. But idiosyncratic trails don't always adhere to ownership boundaries, and many trails cross in and out of private timber land or development tracts. Ownership can change at any time, so if you run into a "No Trespassing" sign, it's time to turn around. In addition, timber harvests on public and private land can decimate trails. Even without the problem of clearcuts, the money pinch on public lands leaves some trails unmaintained. So for many reasons, get in the habit of calling the land manager before heading out.

Land managers don't always like hearing from us, but if they know that mountain bikes account for a large percentage of the use on a trail, they'll have a harder time closing it. Hearing from users and constituents makes a difference. Land managers make major decisions based on public input. Be a squeaky wheel.

Land Managers

King County Parks	(206) 296-4232
Mount St. Helens National Monument	(360) 247-3900
National Forest Service	(206) 470-4060
Gifford Pinchot National Forest	(360) 891-5001
Mount Baker–Snoqualmie National Forest	(425) 775-9702
Olympic National Forest	(360) 956-2400
Wenatchee National Forest	(509) 662-4335
National Park Service	(206) 470-4060
Mountain Rainier National Park	(360) 569-2211
Olympic National Park	(360) 452-4501
Washington State Department of Fish and Wildlife	(360) 902-2200
Washington State Department of Natural Resources (DNR)	(800) 527-3305
Washington State Parks	(800) 233-0321

Political Offices

King County Council	(206) 296-1000
United States House of Representatives	(202) 224-3121
United States Senate	(202) 224-3121
Washington State Legislative Switchboard	(800) 321-2808
White House Switchboard	(202) 456-1414

Clubs

Backcountry Bicycle Trails Club (Seattle)	(206) 283-2995
Cascade Bicycle Club (Seattle)	(206) 522-3222
International Mountain Bike Association (IMBA)	(303) 545-9011
Single Track Mind (Tacoma)	(253) 565-5124
Greatful Tread (Yakima)	(509) 248-5393
Portland United Mountain Pedalers (Portland)	(503) 223-3954

Out Riding: Tips and Techniques

Eating

Eat constantly to avoid the dreaded double-headed bonk. Eating is more important than training and *way* more effective at holding that bonk at bay than all the titanium components your bank account can afford. I usually start out with at least 1,000 calories of food in my pack: candy bars, energy bars, peanuts, Fig Newtons, and at least one piece of fruit to avoid energy-bar stomach, from which no amount of Tums can save you.

Drinking

Always bring plenty of water and drink constantly. Two quarts a day is the minimum. I've quaffed three quarts of water on a really hot day. Eating and drinking enough can get you up a lot of hills.

Walking

Most riders will push their bikes during some part of every ride included in *Mountain Bike!* that is rated three, four, or five wheels. Walking your bike is nothing to be ashamed of—it's part of the sport. Walk to avoid getting hurt, walk to save your legs for the rest of the ride, and walk around muddy areas to save delicate trails.

Cadence

As a rule, it's best to pedal 70 to 100 rotations per minute while riding a bike. This can seem awkwardly fast if you're not used to "spinning." But a healthy cadence is the easiest way to keep your legs fresh for the longest time possible. Slow, laborious pedal strokes strain muscles, tiring them for the miles ahead. On rough trails, the cadence rule doesn't always apply, but it's good to keep in mind in order to stay smooth and loose.

Descents

The header, digger, cartwheel, and flip are bad. Riding sideways toward small children is also bad. Either ride in control or walk down the steep sections. Sit back to lower your center of gravity, and keep your arms and legs slightly bent. Keep your hands firmly and consistently on the brakes; you'll get nowhere waving one arm around like a cowboy. Don't use your front brake suddenly or erratically. The conundrum of braking: The front brake does most of the real braking, but you have more precise steering and you're less likely to take a header if less pressure is applied to the front brake. Remember that speed is the most hazardous bicycling condition—it's difficult to get hurt at 1 mile per hour; at 20 miles per hour, it's all too easy.

Climbs

The idea is to get to the top without hurling. Ride at a pace you can sustain for the length of the climb, concentrating on deep, relaxed breathing. Avoid locomotive breathing. Generally, it's best to stay seated so your rear wheel doesn't spin out. If traction is not a problem, try pedaling in a standing position occasionally to save your butt and utilize different muscles. Remember: It's okay to take a rest break.

Training

Do some. Of course, if you're already out riding, then it's too late for me to do much sermonizing, but you'll have a better time if you've put some miles in before a tough ride. More importantly, carefully select the ride or your riding partner. Don't ride an epic with an über-biker if you'd rather be following first-gear Freddy on a three-wheeler.

Maintenance

You'll have more fun out on the trail if your bike rolls smoothly, doesn't skip gears, and doesn't screech when you brake. Think about it: All week long you have to deal with copy machines that don't copy, computers that crash, and co-workers who skip gears and screech—so doesn't it make sense that when you are spending your own free time, you use something that works the way it's supposed to? Keep your bike in good working order.

1 Packwood Lake

⊛⊛

Distance	8.6 miles
Ride	Out & Back; gated dirt road, wide singletrack; views
Duration	1 to 2 hours
Travel time	Yakima—1.5 hours; Seattle—2.5 hours; Portland—4 hours
Hill factor	Mostly flat with a few short hills; 100-foot gain
Skill level	Beginner
Season	Late spring, summer, fall
Maps	Green Trails: Packwood
Users	Bicyclists, equestrians, hikers
More info	Gifford Pinchot National Forest, Packwood District, 360-494-0600

Packwood Lake

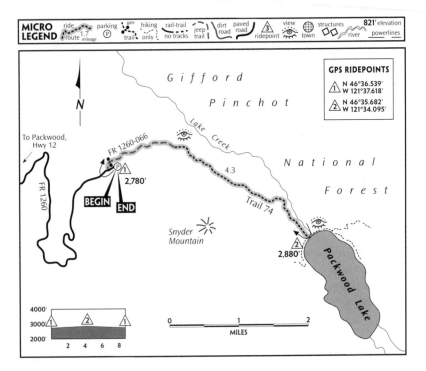

Prelude

The ride to Packwood Lake is an easy ride for families, beginners, or anyone interested in a picnic lunch surrounded by nature's beauty. The ride begins with views of Mount Rainier and ends at pristine Packwood Lake, with upper Lake Creek Valley and the high peaks of Goat Rocks Wilderness beyond. There's no place for fast riding on this wide, sometimes crowded trail; the lack of significant elevation gain helps deter that possibility.

To Get There

Start the odometer in Packwood at the junction of US Highway 12 and Snyder Street, next to the U.S. Forest Service ranger station. Turn east on Snyder Street. At 0.9 mile, Snyder Street becomes Forest Road 1260. Continue up FR 1260 to Packwood Lake Trailhead and parking area at 6 miles.

The Ride

From the parking area at the end of the road, ride back down the paved road toward Packwood. At **0.2** mile, turn right onto the gated service road, FR 066.

Spinning toward Packwood Lake with Mount Rainier in the background

The old dirt road makes a level traverse around the northern flank of Snyder Mountain. At **1.6** miles, take the right fork and ride up a short, rocky hill. From here the road bends east, offering views of the Tatoosh Range and Mount Rainier to the north.

At **3.2** miles, reach a four-way intersection: Go straight, following the "Trail" signs. The trail narrows and enters the woods, passing some big trees; with the exception of a couple short ascents, it continues the traverse toward Packwood Lake. Ignore a fork back to the right at **4.1** miles. At **4.3** miles, arrive at picturesque Packwood Lake. Note that bicycles are not allowed on the trails around the lake. After soaking up the scenery of the lake, Anges Island, and the Goat Rocks Wilderness beyond, turn around and retrace the route back to the parking area, **8.6** miles.

Gazetteer

Nearby camping: La Wis Wis Campground
Nearest food, drink, services: Packwood

2 PACKWOOD
Skate Creek
⊕⊕⊕

Distance	13.1 miles
Ride	Loop; singletrack, dirt road; views
Duration	2 to 3 hours
Travel time	Yakima—2 hours; Seattle—3 hours; Portland—4 hours
Hill factor	Moderate dirt-road climb; 1,460-foot gain
Skill level	Intermediate
Season	Late spring, summer, fall
Maps	U.S. Forest Service: Packwood Ranger District
Users	Bicyclists, equestrians, vehicles on road
More info	Gifford Pinchot National Forest, Packwood District, 360-494-0600

Prelude

A typical dirt-road climb/singletrack descent loop, Skate Creek offers a sustained *ka-pow* view of Mount Rainier as well as a trail off-limits to hikers. I rode this on a particularly clear day in August and was amazed at the vivid

Mount Rainier from Silver Creek Trail

detail I could see of Rainier's southern glaciers. The climb, through clearcuts, is generally moderate with some steep pitches thrown in for good measure; the singletrack is fast, fun, and beautiful.

To Get There

Start the odometer in Packwood at the junction of US Highway 12 and Skate Creek Road near the U.S. Forest Service ranger station. Drive west on Skate Creek Road. Skate Creek Road becomes Forest Road 52. Stay on the main road, which is paved, until you reach FR 5240 on the left, 12.1 miles. Turn left onto FR 5240 and park immediately.

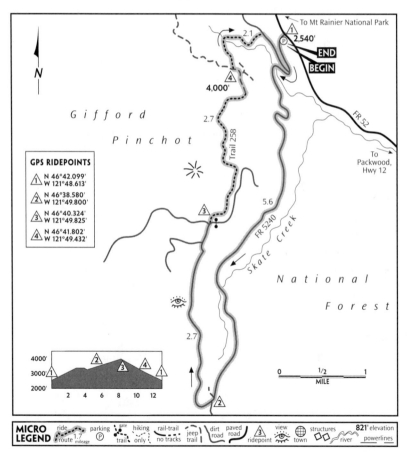

The Ride

From its junction with FR 52, pedal up FR 5240. The dirt road gains altitude quickly. At the first switchback, pass a lesser road on the right and then another on the left. Continue up the main road. Ignore two more spur roads on the right, at **1.9** miles and **2.8** miles. The road levels at **3.2** miles and parallels Skate Creek, which is below on the left.

At **3.8** miles, take the main road, which forks to the left and descends to the creek. Immediately after crossing Skate Creek, bear right at the fork and begin climbing again. At **5.6** miles, ignore a spur to the right that heads toward the deafening roar of many stacked beehives. Just after the bee spur, reach a T: Turn right. The road climbs a short distance, then levels and traverses north, straight at Mount Rainier. The view is so good that on a clear day you can count the number of crevasses in each glacier. Stay on the main road.

Arrive at a fork, **8** miles, and bear right. At the next fork, **8.2** miles, find Silver Creek Trail 258, which exits the intersection between the two roads. According to the sign, hikers are not allowed on this trail. From the start, the trail seems rough and unmaintained, but gradually you'll find that it just doesn't get much use—closed to hikers, too short for motorcyclists, and dangerous for equestrians because mountain beaver keep digging underneath the trail. After the short, rough section of trail, you'll find yourself opening it up, zipping and traversing through an older second-growth forest.

The trail mirrors Silver Creek for a stretch, then bears left. At **10.6** miles, meet a dirt road and go left. Ignore a dirt road that forks back to the right at **10.9** miles. WHOA! At **11** miles, find a wood post marking a faint trail on the right—take this trail. The trail drops sharply, then crosses a small bridge over an unnamed Skate Creek tributary at **11.3** miles. Bear right and follow this stream through thick fern undergrowth. Enter a recent clearcut and switchback down to a dirt road and parking area, **12.1** miles. Turn right and ride down the road to a T at **12.6** miles: Turn left and ride one-half mile back to the parking area near FR 52, **13.1** miles.

Gazetteer

Nearby camping: Longmire Campground, La Wis Wis Campground
Nearest food, drink, services: Packwood

SOUTH OF RANDLE

3 Kraus Ridge

⊕⊕⊕

Distance	5.8 miles
Ride	Loop; singletrack, doubletrack, dirt road
Duration	1 to 2 hours
Travel time	Yakima—2 hours; Seattle—3 hours; Portland—3.5 hours
Hill Factor	Steady, 2-mile dirt-road climb; 600-foot gain
Skill level	Intermediate
Season	Summer, fall
Maps	U.S. Forest Service: Randle Ranger District
Users	Bicyclists, equestrians, hikers
More info	Gifford Pinchot National Forest, Randle District, 360-497-1100

Prelude

My out-of-shape cousin nearly passed out at the top of the two-mile climb that begins this ride. When he lay down on his back in the middle of the old road, I waved peppered beef jerky under his nose to revive him. Then, after

Climbing toward Bluff Mountain

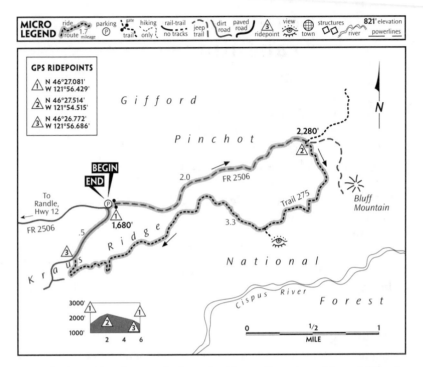

MICRO LEGEND — ride route, 1.7 mileage, parking Ⓟ, gate, hiking trail only, rail-trail no tracks, jeep trail, dirt road, paved road, ③ ridepoint, view, town, structures, river, 821' elevation, powerlines

GPS RIDEPOINTS

△1 N 46°27.081' W 121°56.429'

△2 N 46°27.514' W 121°54.515'

△3 N 46°26.772' W 121°56.686'

we rode down the zippy trail, through old growth and corridors of fern, he wanted to ride the loop again. Go figure. The downhill set a firm smile on his face and the endorphin-packed ascent had produced amnesia.

To Get There

Start the odometer in Randle at the junction of US Highway 12 and State Route 131. Proceed south on SR 131. At 1 mile, take the right fork, following the signs toward Mount St. Helens, on Forest Road 25. At 6.5 miles, turn left on FR 2506. Stay on the main road until you reach the fork of FR 2506 and FR 037 at 8.8 miles. Park at this fork.

The Ride

From the fork of FR 2506 and FR 037, ride left down FR 2506, away from the "Kraus Ridge Trail" sign. The road immediately begins a steep climb toward Bluff Mountain. At **1.2** miles, the road levels somewhat. Ignore a grassy road on the right, **1.6** miles. WHOA! At **2** miles, find the easy-to-miss Kraus Ridge Trail 275, which crosses the road. Turn right onto the trail and climb a short distance.

Last light of day on Trail 275

Soon you'll be winding along a smooth trail through thick old growth. The descent will keep a smile on your face. At **3.2** miles, the trail forks: Bear right to continue (the left fork leads to a great viewpoint high above the Cispus River). After another short climb, the trail drops again, tossing in a couple of switchbacks to this excellent descent. At **5.3** miles, the trail arrives at a dirt road: Turn right. Pedal down the road to the intersection of FR 037 and FR 2506 to complete the loop, **5.8** miles.

Gazetteer
Nearby camping: Iron Creek Campground
Nearest food, drink, services: Randle

SOUTH OF RANDLE

4 Tongue Mountain
⊛⊛⊛

Distance	10.5 miles
Ride	Loop; singletrack, dirt road
Duration	1 to 3 hours
Travel time	Yakima—2 hours; Seattle—3 hours; Portland—3.5 hours
Hill factor	Steady dirt-road climb, 1-mile walk on trail; 1,810-foot gain
Skill level	Advanced
Season	Summer, fall
Maps	Green Trails: McCoy Peak
Users	Bicyclists, equestrians, hikers, motorcyclists
More info	Gifford Pinchot National Forest, Randle District, 360-497-1100

Tongue Mountain Trail, northbound

Prelude

Here's a relatively short ride that combines a dirt-road climb with a fun, yet at times challenging, singletrack descent. I rode the loop on a hot August day and easily went through two quarts of water; there's little shade on the climb. The one-mile push up a steep section of trail adds to the need for sufficient liquid. As on the Kraus Ridge Trail, the fast, forested descent down the out-stretched tongue of Tongue Mountain will make you consider riding the loop a second time.

To Get There

Start the odometer in Randle at the junction of US Highway 12 and State Route 131. Proceed south on SR 131. At 1 mile, take the left fork onto Forest

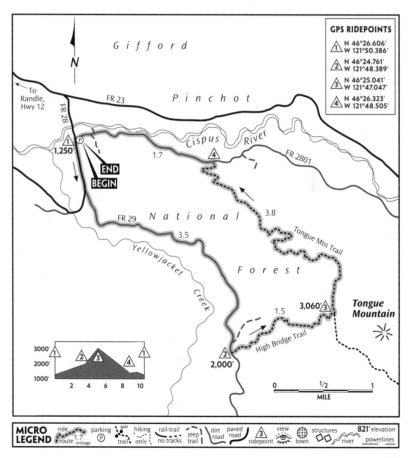

GPS RIDEPOINTS	
1	N 46°26.606' W 121°50.386'
2	N 46°24.761' W 121°48.389'
3	N 46°25.041' W 121°47.047'
4	N 46°26.323' W 121°48.505'

MICRO LEGEND — ride route, 1.7 mileage, parking P, gate, hiking trail, trail only no tracks, rail-trail, jeep trail, dirt road, paved road, ridepoint, view, town, structures, river, 821' elevation, powerlines

Road 23, following signs toward the Cispus Learning Center. Stay on the main paved road. At 9.5 miles, turn right on FR 28 and cross the Cispus River. Just across the river, turn left on FR 2801 and park.

The Ride

From the junction of FR 2801 and FR 28, ride south, away from the Cispus River, on flat, paved FR 28. At **0.5** mile, reach a fork: Turn left onto FR 29. The dirt starts here. Ignore a spur on the left at **0.6** mile. From here the road climbs steadily, rising high above Yellowjacket Creek, which is below on the right. Ignore three more spur roads: on the left at **2.2** miles, on the right at **3.4** miles, and finally on the left at **3.5** miles. Just past the third spur, find High Bridge Trail on the left. Take the trail.

The trail ascends at a steep grade for one-quarter mile, then noodles through the forest to a wet meadow and series of beaver ponds, **4.3** miles. After crossing a short bridge, the trail becomes too steep to ride. Push your bike up the steep, somewhat open hillside. At **5** miles, High Bridge Trail ends at a T: Turn left onto Tongue Mountain Trail. (Tongue Mountain and, later, Juniper Ridge Trail are found to the right.) With 99 percent of the climbing now complete, traverse north to catch a broad ridge that spills to the northwest from Tongue Mountain.

The smooth ridge trail roller-coasters down, becoming steeper at each successive corner. From the **6.2**-mile mark, the trail switchbacks down a precipitous slope. On parts of the descent, the trail is wide, loose, and rocky from motorcycle use. At **8.7** miles, the trail ends at a dirt road. Turn left on the road, FR 2801, and ride along Cispus River to the junction with FR 28, **10.5** miles, to complete the loop.

Gazetteer

Nearby camping: Iron Creek Campground
Nearest food, drink, services: Randle

5 Juniper Ridge Epic

☼☼☼☼☼

Distance	37.1 miles
Ride	Loop; singletrack, dirt road; views
Duration	6 to 9 hours
Travel time	Yakima—2.5 hours; Seattle—3.5 hours; Portland—4 hours
Hill factor	Relentless up and down, some hike-a-bike; 2,920-foot gain
Skill level	Advanced
Season	Late summer, fall
Maps	U.S. Forest Service: Randle Ranger District; Green Trails: McCoy Peak, Blue Lake
Users	Bicyclists, motorcyclists, equestrians, hikers
More info	Gifford Pinchot National Forest, Randle District, 360-497-1100

Still fresh on Boundary Trail 1

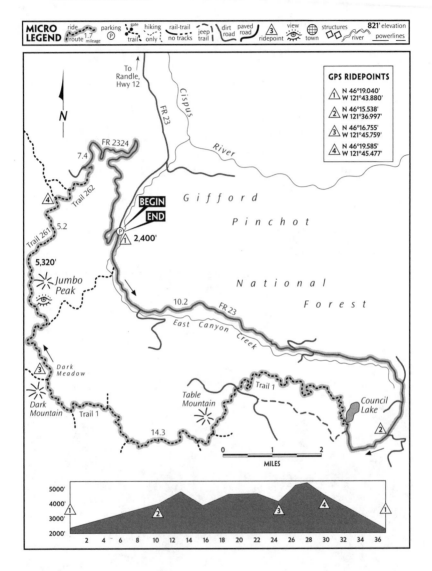

MICRO LEGEND — ride route, 1.7 mileage, parking (P), gate, hiking trail only, rail-trail no tracks, jeep trail, dirt road, paved road, 3 ridepoint, view, town, structures, river, 821' elevation, powerlines

To Randle, Hwy 12

FR 23

Cispus River

FR 2324

7.4

Trail 262

Trail 261   5.2

4

BEGIN
END

P
1 2,400'

Gifford   Pinchot

National   Forest

GPS RIDEPOINTS
1 N 46°19.040'
    W 121°43.880'
2 N 46°15.538'
    W 121°36.997'
3 N 46°16.755'
    W 121°45.759'
4 N 46°19.585'
    W 121°45.477'

5,320'
Jumbo Peak

10.2

FR 23

East Canyon Creek

3 Dark Meadow

Dark Mountain   Trail 1

Table Mountain

Trail 1

Council Lake

2

14.3

0   1   2
MILES

5000'
4000'
3000'
2000'

1   2   3   4   1

2   4   6   8   10 12 14 16 18 20 22 24 26 28 30 32 34 36

Prelude

If some have their way, much of this route would become the Dark Divide Wilderness. That would be a shame for mountain bicyclists because Juniper Ridge Trail is one of the more stunning high-country trails in the south Cascades. A better solution would be a National Recreation Area designation, which would protect this wonderful area while allowing continued bicycle

Heading north along Juniper Ridge with Jumbo Peak ahead

use. Due to several fires early this century, the ridge tops are devoid of trees, offering awesome views: On a clear day, four volcanoes are visible from Juniper Ridge. On the day I passed Jumbo Peak, huckleberry, azalea, and mountain ash lit up the cloudy autumn day with raving yellows and reds. Though I rated this ride five wheels—for the distance, the relentless up and down, and a few dangerous sections—it is one of the more ridable epics included in this book.

To Get There

Start the odometer in Randle at the junction of US Highway 12 and State Route 131. Proceed south on SR 131. At 1 mile, take the left fork onto Forest Road 23, following signs toward the Cispus Learning Center. Stay on the main paved road; at the fork, 19.6 miles, stay to the right on FR 23. At 24.3 miles, find FR 2324 on the right. Park at this fork.

The Ride

From the fork of FR 23 and FR 2324, begin the long dirt-road climb by riding up FR 23. Stay on the main, well-trafficked road during the climb. After mounting some steep corners and passing numerous spurs, reach the inter-section of FR 23 and FR 2334, **10.2** miles. From here, turn right and pedal west on FR 2334 toward Council Lake—stay on the main road. At a fork, **11.4** miles, bear right on FR 016. Reach Council Lake and the small campground at **11.7** miles. Follow the road through the camp area to the start of Boundary Trail 1, an old road. The narrow, rutted road immediately heads up, gaining 600 feet over the next mile. At **13** miles, the old road ends. From here, continue on Boundary Trail 1 to the left, a narrow singletrack that zips across the back flank of Council Bluff before switchbacking down toward Table Creek.

At **15.6** miles, cross Table Creek and begin climbing again. Cross a dirt road, **16.3** miles, and continue the ascent toward Table Mountain on a fine trail. At **18** miles, ignore Boundary Trail 1C, which cuts back to the left. From here the trail is in a constant state of either climbing or descending, through a sparse forest, around rock outcroppings, and past tasty huckleberries. Reach a fork, **18.6** miles, and go right, staying on Boundary Trail 1. After about one mile of likely hike-a-bike, reach Summit Prairie and a fork, **21.1** miles, and bear right. Gradually descend the ridge toward Dark Mountain in the distance. At **22** miles, take the left fork. While noodling through a high meadow near the **23**-mile point, again take the right fork.

Soon after, the trail bends north and climbs a bit before dropping into Dark Meadow. At **24.5** miles, arrive at a fork: Go right, on Juniper Ridge Trail 261. The route continues northward, bounded by Dark Mountain to the south and Jumbo Peak to the north. At **25.6** miles, reach another fork and go left. From here the trail climbs at a steep rate, making much of the next mile a push. From the **26.5**-mile point to the ridge top at **27.1** miles, the trail isn't as steep, but this section is still a hike-a-bike. As the trail continues along the top of the ridge toward Jumbo Peak, the awesome four-volcano view—Rainier, Adams, St. Helens, Hood—may inspire religious conversion.

At **27.8** miles, crest the ride's high point as you cross over the west shoulder of Jumbo Peak. Drop quickly down the sometimes-rocky trail to a fork at **29.7** miles. Turn right on Sunrise Trail, following the signs toward FR 2324. After a short climb, pass a trail going up on the left, then descend down a steep slope to FR 2324, **31.1** miles. Glide down the dirt road to a fork at **31.4** miles: Take the right fork. Continue the descent to a T at **32.6** miles: Go left. After several long, fast switchbacks, arrive at FR 23 to complete the loop, **37.1** miles.

Gazetteer

Nearby camping: Takhlakh Lake Campground, Blue Creek Campground
Nearest food, drink, services: Randle

SOUTH OF RANDLE

6 High Lakes

✤✤✤

Distance	18.2 miles
Ride	Loop; singletrack, dirt road, 2 miles paved road; views
Duration	2 to 4 hours
Travel time	Yakima—2.5 hours; Seattle—3.5 hours; Portland—4 hours
Hill factor	Continuous up and down, some walking; 1,240-foot gain
Skill level	Advanced
Season	Summer, fall
Maps	U.S. Forest Service: Randle Ranger District
Users	Bicyclists, equestrians, hikers, motorcyclists
More info	Gifford Pinchot National Forest, Randle District, 360-497-1100

Adams Creek

Mount Adams from Takh Takh Meadows

Prelude

With much of this ride following the dirt roads near Takhlakh Lake, and a mere 1,000-foot elevation gain, it is a pretty plush three-wheeler. In addition, only one section of the trail (the one I took a header on) requires much riding skill. However, the climb out of the Adams Creek valley is a likely hike-a-bike. And then there's the problem with Adams Creek: It runs directly out from under Adams Glacier and, because of this, the creek's milky consistency obscures the creek's bed. I can assure you that it's deeper than it looks, even in late August (though I wasn't forced to "Wynooch" it, as in Ride 59). Lots of equestrians use this trail system, so even though some of the sections are extremely fun, be sure to yield to all other trail users.

To Get There

Start the odometer in Randle at the junction of US Highway 12 and State Route 131. Drive south on SR 131. At 1 mile, take the left fork onto Forest Road 23. Stay on the main paved road; at the fork, 19.6 miles, bear right, staying on FR 23. The road soon becomes gravel. Continue to 32.8 miles and turn left on FR 2329 toward Takhlakh Lake. At 33.6 miles, take the right fork, staying on FR 2329. At 34 miles, turn left on FR 022 toward Chain of Lakes. The road ends at High Lakes Trailhead, 35.1 miles. Park here.

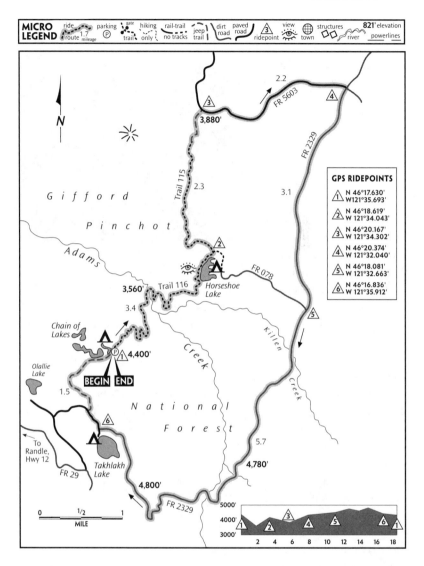

The Ride

Start by pedaling up High Lakes Trail 116. After a short climb, the trail switch-backs down a steep slope into the Adams Creek valley. At **1.7** miles, it's time to ford Adams Creek. **WHOA!** The glacier-fed creek is freezing, milky, and deceptively deep. From the creek, the trail charges up the opposite side of the valley, requiring some hike-a-bike until leveling out at the **2.5**-mile mark.

Quickly cross a second creek and grind up another slope to Horseshoe Lake. From the shore, check out Mount Adams, which caps the lake like an old Bell helmet.

One of the Chain Lakes

Reach a T at **3.4** miles: Turn left onto Spring Creek Trail. From here, the smooth, compact, spry trail winds downward toward FR 5603. This is a heavily used trail, so keep your speed down and ride in control. At **4.3** miles, the trail forks: Go right. When the trail ends at a doubletrack, **5.1** miles, bear right. Pedal along the doubletrack to paved FR 5603, at **5.7** miles. Turn right and ride up the road. It's a stiff climb, but the pavement mitigates the pain. At a four-way intersection, **7.9** miles, turn right onto FR 2329 toward Horseshoe Lake. Stay on the main road, passing several lesser roads on either side, as you gradually climb. At **11** miles, pass the road to Horseshoe Lake, FR 078, on the right.

From here, FR 2329 careens up and down, through a pretty pine forest that affords occasional views of Mount Adams and Mount Rainier. Again, stay on the main road. Just beyond the 16-mile point, pass Takh Takh Meadows on the right. When the road forks at **16.7** miles, go right. At **17** miles, turn right onto FR 022 toward Chain of Lakes. Climb for just less than one-half mile, then descend down the narrow road past Chain of Lakes Campground to High Lakes Trailhead to complete the loop, **18.2** miles.

Gazetteer

Nearby camping: Chain of Lakes Campground
Nearest food, drink, services: Randle

7

SOUTH OF RANDLE

Horseshoe Lake
◈◈

Distance	9.3 miles
Ride	Loop; singletrack, dirt road, paved road; views
Duration	2 to 3 hours
Travel time	Yakima—2.5 hours; Seattle—3.5 hours; Portland—4 hours
Hill factor	2 miles moderate paved-road climbing; 620-foot gain
Skill level	Beginner
Season	Summer, fall
Maps	U.S. Forest Service: Randle Ranger District
Users	Bicyclists, equestrians, hikers, motorcyclists
More info	Gifford Pinchot National Forest, Randle District, 360-497-1100

Prelude

This is a perfect ride for first-time singletrackers or those curious to see what mountain biking is all about. The singletrack section is easy (except for the first quarter mile of the ride, which is flat but somewhat rough) and relatively short. Most of the trail is zippy and fun. Watch out for other trail users, especially equestrians. The rest of the route traverses roads, both dirt and paved, and requires little riding skill, though the climb up a paved road requires some effort.

To Get There

Start the odometer in Randle at the junction of US Highway 12 and State Route 131. Drive south on SR 131. At 1 mile, take the left fork onto Forest Road 23. Depending on current roadwork on FR 23, the pavement ends at around 20 miles. Continue up FR 23 to 32.8 miles, then turn left on FR 2329 toward Takhlakh Lake. At 33.6 miles, take the right fork, staying on FR 2329. At 34.3 miles, turn left and follow FR 2329 to its junction with FR 078, at 40 miles. Turn left on FR 078 and proceed to Horseshoe Lake Campground, 41.5 miles. Park here.

Cruising Trail 115 near Horseshoe Lake

The Ride

Take the narrow trail that exits from campsite 5 at Horseshoe Lake Camp-ground. The trail wraps around the east end of the lake. For beginners, this short section may require a walk. Ignore three trails that come in quick succession on the right. At a fork at **0.2** mile, bear right, onto Spring Creek Trail 115. From here, the smooth, compact trail—excellent for beginning single-trackers—winds downward toward FR 5603. At **1.1** miles, the trail forks: Go right. When the trail ends at a doubletrack, **1.9** miles, bear right. Pedal easily down the doubletrack to paved FR 5603, at **2.5** miles. Turn right and ride up the road. It's a stiff climb up the road, but the pavement makes the riding easier and lessens the pain. At a four-way intersection, **4.7** miles, turn right onto FR 2329 toward Horseshoe Lake. Stay on the main road as you gradually climb. At **7.8** miles, turn right onto FR 078 toward Horseshoe Lake. **WHOA!**

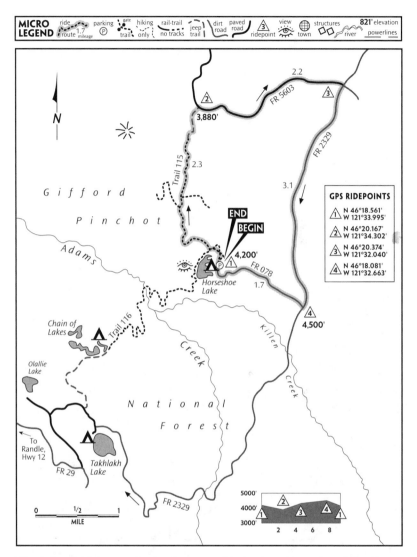

MICRO LEGEND: ride route 1.7 mileage • parking ℗ • gate • hiking trail • rail-trail no tracks • jeep trail • dirt road • paved road • ③ ridepoint • view • town • structures • river • 821' elevation • powerlines

GPS RIDEPOINTS

⚠ N 46°18.561'
W 121°33.995'

② N 46°20.167'
W 121°34.302'

③ N 46°20.374'
W 121°32.040'

④ N 46°18.081'
W 121°32.663'

Watch for vehicles on the road as you ride back to Horseshoe Lake Campground, **9.3** miles.

Gazetteer

Nearby camping: Horseshoe Lake Campground
Nearest food, drink, services: Randle

8 SOUTH OF RANDLE
Three Buttes
⚙⚙⚙

Distance	18 miles
Ride	Loop; dirt road, doubletrack, some singletrack; views
Duration	2 to 5 hours
Travel time	Yakima—2 hours; Seattle—3 hours; Portland—3.5 hours
Hill factor	Moderate 12-mile climb with steep sections; 1,660-foot gain
Skill level	Intermediate
Season	Summer, fall
Maps	U.S. Forest Service: Randle Ranger District
Users	Bicyclists, motorcycles, vehicles on road
More info	Gifford Pinchot National Forest, Randle District, 360-497-1100

Mount Adams from Forest Road 77

Prelude

With just one mile of singletrack over the entire route, I expected this to be a simple dirt-road ride—enjoyable and even fun, but without the excitement of extended miles of singletrack. Antidote: perfect views of Mount St. Helens, Mount Adams, and Mount Rainier from one spot along the ride. The beautifully flowered subalpine meadows and hearty fir forests don't hurt either.

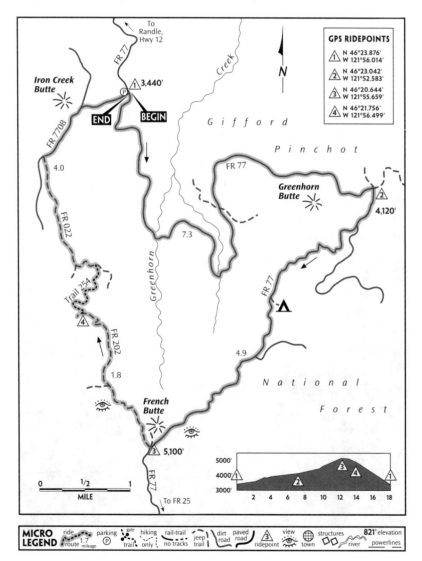

To Randle, Hwy 12

FR 77

Creek

N

GPS RIDEPOINTS

△1 N 46°23.876'
W 121°56.014'

△2 N 46°23.042'
W 121°52.583'

△3 N 46°20.644'
W 121°55.659'

△4 N 46°21.756'
W 121°56.499'

Iron Creek Butte

△1 3,440'

FR 7708

END   BEGIN

G i f f o r d

P i n c h o t

FR 77

4.0

Greenhorn Butte

△2

4,120'

FR 022

7.3

Trail 254

Greenhorn

FR 77

△4

Λ

FR 202

4.9

1.8

N a t i o n a l

French Butte

F o r e s t

△3 5,100'

FR 77

0   1/2   1
MILE

To FR 25

5000'
4000' △1
3000'

△3
△2   △4
△1

2 4 6 8 10 12 14 16 18

MICRO LEGEND ride route 1.7 mileage | parking P | gate, hiking trail only | rail-trail no tracks | jeep trail | dirt road | paved road | △3 ridepoint | view | town | structures | river | 821' elevation | powerlines

Though the dirt road climbs for twelve miles, much of it consists of a gradual, undulating traverse on smooth roads (of course, some of the steep sections require your lowest gear). The access road to the starting point—beneath Tower Rock and switchbacking up Forest Road 77—counts as one of the intrigues of this ride.

To Get There

Start the odometer in Randle at the junction of US Highway 12 and State Route 131. Go south on SR 131. At 1 mile, take the left fork onto Forest Road 23, following signs toward the Cispus Learning Center. At 9.5 miles, turn right on FR 28 (Cispus Road) and cross the Cispus River. At 10.9 miles, take the right fork, remaining on FR 28. At 12.5 miles, turn left on FR 76; take the left fork again at 13.2 miles. At 15.3 miles, turn left on FR 77. At 23.1 miles, park at the intersection of FR 77 and FR 7708 on the right.

The Ride

From the intersection of FR 77 and FR 7708, near Iron Creek Butte, pedal out on FR 77. Washboarded at times, the gravelly road traverses the flats between Iron Creek Butte and Greenhorn Butte. Stay on the main road, climbing gradually. After winding into and back out of three creeks, the road climbs more

Climbing toward French Butte

steadily up the north base of Greenhorn Butte to a saddle at **7.2** miles. At the saddle, ignore all three dirt roads on the left, following the main road, FR 77, around to the right toward Pole Patch. When confronted, at **7.7** miles, with a three-pointed, tridentlike fork, take the middle road, again following the signs toward Pole Patch on FR 77.

The road narrows somewhat, gradually ascending toward the southwest. At **9.6** miles, pass the entrance to Pole Patch Campground on the left. The smooth dirt road continues climbing the ridgeline. Around the **10**-mile point, the pleasant pine forest abates as open meadows and the steep slopes of the ridge offer spectacular views of Mount Rainier to the north and, soon after, Mount Adams to the south. At a fork, **10.2** miles, bear right. After a number of tight, twisting switchbacks around rocky escarpments and a long south-facing traverse, arrive at the high point of the ride, located below the south corner of French Butte, **12.2** miles.

A jeep trail on the right, FR 201, leads to the top of French Butte, though trees obscure any panoramic view. Instead, take the second right and ride north on FR 202, which traverses high above Iron Creek and affords views of Mount St. Helens. (**WHOA!** This is an easy turn to miss.) FR 202, rutted, narrow, and more primitive than the other roads on this ride, descends to a fork at **13.1** miles: Stay to the right, following signs for Trail 254. From here, the road eases down the ridge. At **14** miles, find French Butte Trail 254 on the right. The trail, faint at first, bears left, then widens and switchbacks down the forested hillside at an exciting rate.

When the trail ends at a road, **15** miles, turn left. At **15.3** miles, bear to the right, staying on the main road. Reach a T at **16.7** miles: Turn right onto FR 1708. Descend to a fork at **17.4** miles: Go right again, staying on FR 1708. Drop to the junction of FR 1708 and FR 77 at **18** miles to complete the loop.

Gazetteer

Nearby camping: Iron Creek Campground
Nearest food, drink, services: Randle

9 Badger Ridge

✿✿✿✿

Distance	15 miles
Ride	Loop; singletrack, dirt road; views
Duration	3 to 5 hours
Travel time	Yakima—2.5 hours; Portland—3 hours; Seattle—3.5 hours
Hill factor	Long dirt-road climb, 1-mile hike-a-bike on trail; 1,760-foot gain
Skill level	Advanced
Season	Summer, fall
Maps	U.S. Forest Service: Randle Ranger District; Green Trails: McCoy Peak
Users	Bicyclists, equestrians, hikers, motorcyclists
More info	Gifford Pinchot National Forest, Randle District, 360-497-1100

Prelude

I thought one of the rules was that it wasn't supposed to rain in August in western Washington. Well, before riding Badger Ridge, we sat in the car for a long time at the Elk Pass trailhead and watched rain slide down the windshield. But we rallied and we were happy we did, because even in the drizzle and mist this is a beautiful ride past rocky cliffs and high meadows. On the way to Badger Pass, we picked huckleberries and stored them in empty water bottles. We noticed a lot of bear scat and

Walking up Trail 257 to Badger Pass

previously munched huckleberry bushes, so we sang songs to warn the bears that we were around while we pushed our bikes up Badger Ridge Trail. The walk is quite strenuous but fairly short; the rest of the route is ridable.

To Get There

Start the odometer in Randle at the junction of US Highway 12 and State Route 131. Proceed south on SR 131. At 1 mile, take the right fork, following the signs toward Mount St. Helens on Forest Road 25. Pass Iron Creek Campground on the left, 10.1 miles. At the fork, 20.8 miles, of FR 25 and FR 99, bear left, staying on FR 25. Continue on FR 25 to Boundary Trail trailhead parking at Elk Pass, 24.8 miles.

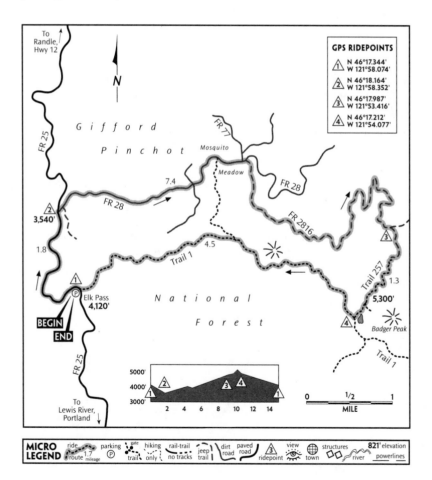

The Ride

From the trailhead at Elk Pass, ride down FR 25 toward Randle to the north. After a fast, paved descent, turn right on FR 28, which is dirt, at **1.8** miles. Ignore a spur on the right, **1.9** miles. The road climbs gradually. At **3.6** miles, ignore dirt roads on the left and right. Pass Mosquito Meadows Trail on the right at **4.2** miles. After another short climb, descend to a four-way intersection at **4.8** miles: Turn right onto FR 2816 toward Badger Ridge Trail. Immediately, the road becomes narrow, rough, and rutted as it climbs away from Mosquito Meadows and onto Badger Peak.

The road zigzags steeply up between rocky cliffs and sloping huckleberry meadows. The way levels just prior to the **9**-mile mark, then descends to a fork at **9.2** miles. Turn right, remaining on FR 2816 toward Badger Ridge Trail. The narrow, rocky trail begins at the end of the road, **9.6** miles, then traverses some cliffs before heading up to the pass at a hectic rate that requires walking. It's strenuous, but a walk through high huckleberries and wild-flowered meadows is wonderful, even on a rainy day. Though you crest Badger Pass at **10.1** miles, the walking may not be over: The first one-quarter mile off the top is nearly straight down. If you do decide to launch, do not skid or run anybody off the trail, or evil mountain bike genies will make thorn magnets out of your tires.

At a T, **10.2** miles, turn right. At **10.5** miles, reach another T and turn right onto Boundary Trail 1. Ride into a deeper forest, down the soft trail that corkscrews and drops off occasional root ledges. At a fork, **12.4** miles, go left. From here the trail roller-coasters—generally down—until it arrives at a paved road, FR 25. Turn right on the road and then, almost immediately, left into the Elk Pass parking area to complete the loop, **15** miles.

Gazetteer

Nearby camping: Iron Creek Campground
Nearest food, drink, services: Randle

10 MOUNT ST. HELENS
Norway Pass
☸☸☸

Distance	11.6 miles
Ride	Loop; singletrack, paved road; views
Duration	1 to 3 hours
Travel time	Yakima—2.5 hours; Portland—3 hours; Seattle—3.5 hours
Hill factor	Moderate up and down with a few steeper climbs; 740-foot gain
Skill level	Intermediate
Season	Summer, fall
Maps	Green Trails: Spirit Lake
Users	Bicyclists, hikers
More info	Mount St. Helens National Monument, 360-247-3900

Ghost Lake

Prelude

Boundary Trail 1 is generally in good shape—cleared of blowdown, smooth and compact—by midsummer. As with all trails, it's prudent to call ahead and ask if this trail has been maintained for the season. This route is ridable just about the entire way; the views of Mount St. Helens are spectacular. The most interesting aspect of this ride, however, is that it teeter-totters between past and present, between a typical western Washington forest and the Mount St. Helens blast zone. A dirt trail and large fir distinguish one side of the ridge, while on the other side, a pumice trail winds through gray, branchless, decapitated tree trunks.

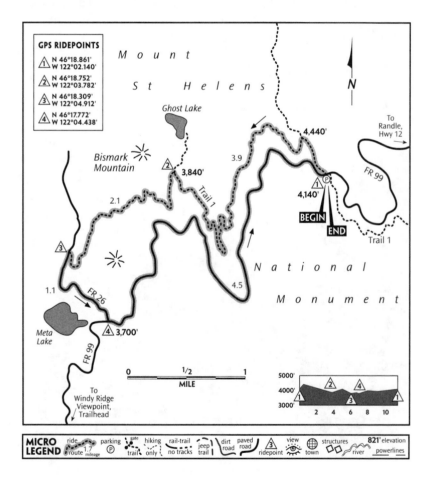

To Get There

Start the odometer in Randle at the junction of US Highway 12 and State Route 131. Proceed south on SR 131. At 1 mile, take the right fork, following the signs toward Mount St. Helens on Forest Road 25. Pass Iron Creek Campground on the left, 10.1 miles. At the fork at 20.8 miles, turn right on FR 99 toward Bear Meadow and Windy Ridge. At 25.6 miles, find the Bear Meadow Interpretive Site on the left. Park here.

The Ride

From the paved parking area at Bear Meadow, carefully cross FR 99 to the trail on

Entering the blast zone

the opposite side of the road. The trail follows the road, then cuts away into the forest and traces a difficult ascent to a T at **0.5** mile. Turn left and traverse the side of a steep ridge. Just before the **3**-mile point, the surroundings begin to change from normal forest to Mount St. Helens blast zone, a surreal landscape of gray, decapitated trees and fine-pumice trail.

With the transformation complete, the trail switchbacks down a hillside toward Bismark Mountain. Gray trees are scattered everywhere as a reminder of the unbelievable power of the 1980 eruption. In a swale between the ridge and Bismark Mountain, reach a fork at **3.9** miles. Turn left and begin climbing. (One-half mile down the right fork, you'll find Ghost Lake, an interesting if somewhat lifeless spot.) The trail winds up to a saddle at **4.9** miles, then switchbacks down to a paved road, **6** miles. Turn left on the road.

The paved road climbs and drops, climbs and finally drops to a T at FR 99, **7.1** miles. Turn left and pedal toward Bear Meadow. Ride carefully on this busy road, usually packed with Mount St. Helens rubberneckers. The road heads up and down, though mostly up, to the parking area at Bear Meadow, **11.6** miles, to complete the loop.

Gazetteer

Nearby camping: Iron Creek Campground
Nearest food, drink, services: Randle

11 Smith Creek Epic

◎◎◎◎◎

Distance	27.4 miles
Ride	Loop; singletrack, dirt road, paved road; views
Duration	6 to 10 hours
Travel time	Yakima—2.5 hours; Portland—3 hours; Seattle—3.5 hours
Hill factor	Strenuous climbs and descents, lots of hike-a-bike; 2,640-foot gain
Skill level	Advanced
Season	Summer, fall
Maps	Green Trails: Spirit Lake, Mount St. Helens
Users	Bicyclists, hikers
More info	Mount St. Helens National Monument, 360-247-3900

Surfing the pumice slopes above Smith Creek

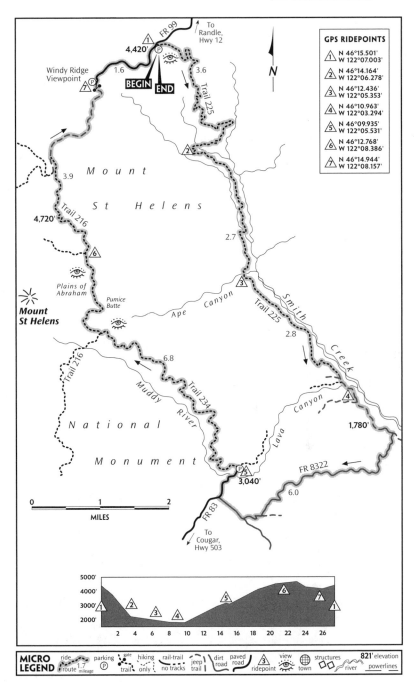

GPS RIDEPOINTS

△	
1	N 46°15.501' W 122°07.003'
2	N 46°14.164' W 122°06.278'
3	N 46°12.436' W 122°05.353'
4	N 46°10.963' W 122°03.294'
5	N 46°09.935' W 122°05.531'
6	N 46°12.768' W 122°08.386'
7	N 46°14.944' W 122°08.157'

To Randle, Hwy 12

FR 99

4,420'

BEGIN END

Windy Ridge Viewpoint

1.6

3.6

Trail 225

N

3.9

Mount

St Helens

4,720'

Trail 216

2.7

Plains of Abraham

Pumice Butte

Mount St Helens

Ape Canyon

Smith Creek

Trail 225

2.8

6.8

Trail 234

Muddy River

Trail 216

Lava Canyon

4

1,780'

National

Monument

3,040'

FR 8322

6.0

FR 83

To Cougar, Hwy 503

0   1   2
MILES

MICRO LEGEND — ride route, 1.7 mileage, parking P, gate, hiking trail, rail-trail no tracks, jeep trail, dirt road, paved road, view ridepoint, town, structures, river, 821' elevation, powerlines

35

Prelude

Much more bushwhacking adventure than simple mountain bike ride, the Smith Creek epic challenges your riding and orienteering skills, your stamina, and any friendships you thought you had with your riding partners. The trail begins by heading down a steep ridge composed of unstable pumice. Soon you will understand what local mountain bikers are talking about when they refer to "surfing the pum." By midafternoon on the day I rode this route, we had already applied first aid to numerous pum cuts, filtered more water out of a Smith Creek tributary to refill our bottles, forded several large creeks—and we hadn't even begun the climb back out. Not long afterward, we were eating racks of Fig Newtons like they were M&Ms and nervously glancing at our watches. Luckily we had lights, so that riding the knife-edge ridge in twilight was fun rather than dangerous. PEFS (post-epic fatigue syndrome) rating: high.

To Get There

Zero the odometer in Randle at the junction of US Highway 12 and State Route 131. Go south on SR 131. At 1 mile, take the right fork, following the signs toward Mount St. Helens on Forest Road 25. Pass Iron Creek Campground on the left, 10.1 miles. At the fork at 20.8 miles, turn right on FR 99 toward Windy Ridge. Just past the 35-mile point, find parking for the Smith Creek trailhead on the left.

The Ride

From the trailhead at the top of the Smith Creek drainage, take a good long look downstream at your hike-a-bike future. If you are still inclined to surf the pum down into Smith Creek (and then pedal back out), go back to your car and load up on more energy bars, warm clothes, and a flashlight for good measure (even though you're making a decision that doesn't make much good sense). With a few more racks of fig bars in tow, start down Smith Creek Trail 225 on an easy traverse that belies the radical drop-off that lurks around the first corner.

Serious pum surfing and switchbacking hike-a-bike begin as the trail careens down the wide ridge toward the creek. In some sections the trail is distinct, compact, and ridable; in others, no trail seems to exist as wands and red flagging guide you through dense shrubbery and across washouts. Near the valley floor on a long, westward traverse, the trail becomes even more difficult to follow despite the flagging. Stick with it and you will eventually

Scenic rest break on Smith Creek Trail 225

find wood posts that mark the route across the small middle fork of Smith Creek, **3.6** miles.

Across the creek, find the faint trail and bear left, riding down the long rise between the two forks of Smith Creek. Use the tall wood posts to follow the trail, which is sometimes obvious and fast, other times difficult to follow and slow. At **5.1** miles, the trail abandons the rise between forks, bearing right and crossing Smith Creek's west fork. **WHOA!** From here the trail is again difficult to follow. Across the creek, bear left and hike-a-bike south. With luck you will soon find the trail. At **6.3** miles, the trail crosses Ape Canyon Creek. Watch the route carefully: It is crucial to cross at the correct spot so you can find the trail that heads away from the creek, climbing. Hike-a-bike to the **6.7**-mile point.

From here, the trail opens up and becomes considerably more ridable. At around **8** miles the trail again climbs away from Smith Creek. At **8.4** miles, the trail widens to become an old road. Follow the road down, ignoring both a spur road and then Trail 184, both on the right. Continue down the road to the creek that flows out of Lava Canyon. Only half the bridge remains—a washout—requiring a dangerous ford. From the opposite side, ride down the road, FR 8322, passing a gravel parking area and a lesser spur road on the right.

At **9.7** miles, the low point of the ride, FR 8322 bears right and begins climbing out of the Smith Creek valley. The road heads up at a steady climb.

Pass a spur road on the left at **10.3** miles. At **13.6** miles, ignore a spur back to the left. When you reach a T at **13.9** miles, turn right. At **14.4** miles, reach another T—turn right on paved FR 83. The paved road drops, crosses the appropriately named Muddy River, and ends at Ape Canyon Trailhead.

From the trailhead, pedal up Ape Canyon Trail 234, tracing the east edge of a gigantic mudflow. After some relatively easy twists and turns, the trail enters a forest of big trees and mounts a ridge that—amazingly—escaped much of the St. Helens eruption unscathed. The trail, steep and unrelenting though smooth and ridable, switchbacks up the ridge through a seemingly normal forest. However, occasional views off the ridge of trees strewn like matchsticks and huge, gray mudflows prove how anomalous this small patch of forest is so close to Mount St. Helens.

By the **19**-mile mark, most of the difficult climbing is over. At **19.6** miles, stop to appreciate the haunting views of the mountain above and Ape Canyon below. Reach a fork, **20.1** miles, and bear right. Soon after, the trail bends north and enters the Plains of Abraham, a gigantic pumice shoulder on the east side of Mount St. Helens, which is peppered with black rocks that seem to float in the pumice like miniature icebergs. The trail across the Plains of Abe is fun and quick with some ups and downs; watch out for other trail users and yield to them all. At **21.9** miles, the trail forks: Go right.

The trail traverses, winding in and out of several drainages before emerging at the top of a knife-edged ridge, **23.2** miles. The trail mimics the top of the ridge as it heads down. You will need to carry your bike down several sets of stairs that begin at **23.5** miles. After negotiating the stairs, continue down the ridge top. At **24** miles, reach a dirt road and turn right. Climb up this gated dirt road toward Windy Ridge Viewpoint. At **25.8** miles, arrive at the viewpoint parking area. Bear to the right on the paved road, FR 99, and continue the ascent back up to Smith Creek trailhead on the right, **27.4** miles, to complete the loop.

Gazetteer

Nearby camping: Iron Creek Campground
Nearest food, drink, services: Randle

MOUNT ST. HELENS
12 Plains of Abraham
⊕⊕⊕

Distance	11.6 miles
Ride	Out & Back; singletrack, gated dirt road; views
Duration	2 to 3 hours
Travel time	Portland—2 hours; Yakima—2.5 hours; Seattle—3.5 hours
Hill factor	A few steep climbs, short walk up stairs; 520-foot gain
Skill level	Intermediate
Season	Summer, fall
Maps	Green Trails: Mount St. Helens
Users	Bicyclists, hikers
More info	Mount St. Helens National Monument, 360-247-3900

Crossing the lunar-like Plains of Abraham

Prelude

Noted for unequivocal views of Mount St. Helens, this ride is a must for any visitor. After a short ride on a gated dirt road, the trail heads up a sharp ridge toward Sasquatch Steps and a frontal-attack view of the mountain. Stairs and a steep trail force a short but vigorous hike-a-bike. During busy summer months, lots of hikers use this incredible, delicate trail: Yield to everyone,

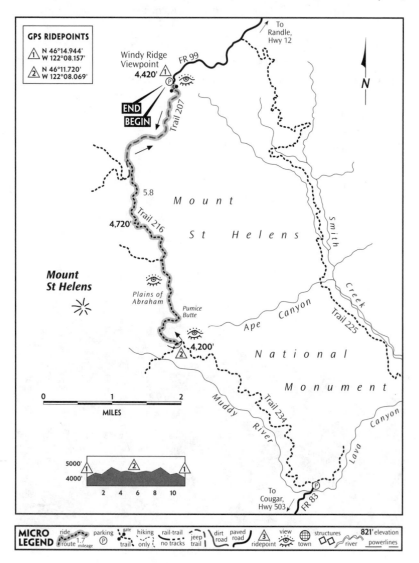

ride in control, and don't leave the trail. The Mount St. Helens National Monument has closed many other trails to mountain bikes. Don't be the reason this one gets closed.

To Get There

Start the odometer in Randle at the junction of US Highway 12 and State Route 131. Go south on SR 131. At 1 mile, take the right fork, following the signs toward Mount St. Helens on Forest Road 25. Pass Iron Creek Campground on the left, 10.1 miles. At the fork at 20.8 miles, turn right on FR 99 toward Windy Ridge. After a lot of winding road and gawking at the blast zone, arrive at the end of the road, 36.5 miles, and the Windy Ridge Viewpoint and trailhead.

South on Trail 216

The Ride

From the parking area at Windy Ridge Viewpoint, begin by riding up the gated, dirt road. A high point is reached at **1.1** miles. Glide down the road to Abraham Trail on the left at **1.8** miles. **WHOA!** This odd, ridge-top trail is easy to miss from the road. Ride up the trail, climbing the blade of a knife-edged ridge. At **2.1** miles, begin walking up a series of steps that climb for about one-quarter mile. From the top of the stairs, continue up the ridge, a possible hike-a-bike.

At **2.6** miles, the trail bears left and leaves the ridgetop, traversing in and out of sharp drainages toward the Plains of Abe. The eerie landscape of broken trees and pumice plains doesn't look much like Washington State. Drop down to an intermittent stream; cairns mark the route. At a fork, **4** miles, bear left on Ape Canyon Trail. From here, the Plains of Abraham spread out ahead; Mount St. Helens dominates the lunar-like landscape. Pedal south toward Pumice Butte along the smooth, compact trail. At **5.8** miles, reach another fork. Turn around here and pedal back to Windy Ridge Viewpoint, **11.6** miles.

Gazetteer

Nearby camping: Iron Creek Campground
Nearest food, drink, services: Randle

13 | MOUNT ST. HELENS
Ape Canyon
❀❀❀❀

Distance	21.6 miles
Ride	Out & Back; singletrack, gated dirt road; views
Duration	3 to 5 hours
Travel time	Portland—1.5 hours; Seattle—3.5 hours
Hill factor	Tough singletrack climb, short walk up stairs; 1,720-foot gain
Skill level	Intermediate
Season	Summer, fall
Maps	Green Trails: Mount St. Helens
Users	Bicyclists, hikers
More info	Mount St. Helens National Monument, 360-247-3900

Prelude

Ape Canyon Trail provides a grueling but ridable climb up to the Plains of Abraham, located on the east flank of Mount St. Helens. The contrast between the forested Ape Canyon Trail and the lunar landscape of the Plains of Abe is unbelievably striking. Pedal from dark green old growth to a gray landscape of pumice and mudflows. At the top, the pumice trail darts across the high plain. It's fun, but watch for other trail users. One of my riding part-

Muddy River valley from Ape Canyon Trail 234

ners took a header into the pum because he was admiring Mount Adams in the distance. Better to stop to soak in the remarkable views.

To Get There

From Interstate 5 at Woodland, drive east on State Route 503, also called Lewis River Road. From the town of Yale, continue east on Lewis River Road

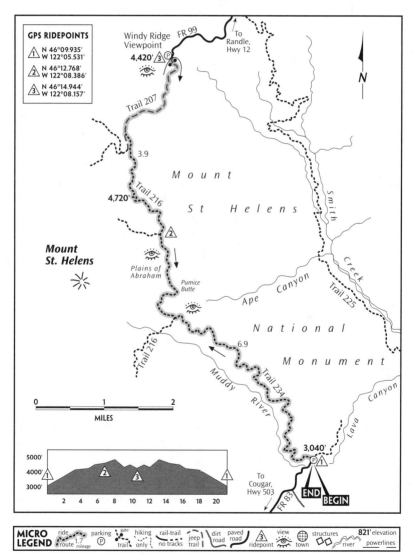

GPS RIDEPOINTS

1 N 46°09.935'
  W 122°05.531'

2 N 46°12.768'
  W 122°08.386'

3 N 46°14.944'
  W 122°08.157'

Windy Ridge Viewpoint   FR 99   To Randle, Hwy 12
4,420' 3

Trail 207

3.9

M o u n t

Trail 216
4,720'

2

S t   H e l e n s

*Mount
St. Helens*

Plains of Abraham

Pumice Butte

Ape   Canyon

Smith Creek

Trail 225

N a t i o n a l

Trail 216

6.9

Trail 234

M o n u m e n t

Lava Canyon

Muddy River

0   1   2
MILES

3,040'

To Cougar, Hwy 503

FR 83   END   BEGIN

5000'
4000' 1   2   3   1
3000'
2 4 6 8 10 12 14 16 18 20

MICRO LEGEND ride route 1.7 mileage | parking P | gate | hiking trail | rail-trail only | jeep no tracks trail | dirt road | paved road | 3 ridepoint | view | structures town | 821' elevation | river powerlines

toward the town of Cougar. Start your odometer in Cougar, and continue east on Lewis River Road, which soon becomes Forest Road 90. At about 7 miles, turn left on FR 83. Take FR 83 to the end, about 18 miles, where you'll find the trailhead parking for Ape Canyon Trail.

The Ride

From the trailhead, pedal into the woods on a nice singletrack—Ape Canyon Trail 234. After some relatively easy twists and turns in a scattered forest, with Muddy River to the left, the trail enters a deeper forest of big trees. The trail gets steeper, climbing a ridge that somehow escaped much of the St. Helens eruption. The trail—steep and grueling—switchbacks up the ridge through a normal-seeming forest. However, occasional vistas to the east and west reveal trees strewn like matchsticks and huge mudflows. It's amazing this ridge survived the 1980 eruption.

By **3.4** miles, most of the difficult climbing is over. With Ape Canyon below to the right and Mount St. Helens looming up to the left, the views at the **4.6**-mile mark are striking and spare. Reach a fork, **5.1** miles, and bear right. Soon after, the trail bends north and crosses the Plains of Abraham, a large pumice shoulder on the east side of Mount St. Helens. The plains are peppered with black rocks and garnished with tiny flowers—the first floral pioneers since the eruption. Be sure to stay on the trail and do not disturb the delicate growth. Long sight distances and a compact tread make the trail across the Plains of Abe zippy and fun; watch out for other trail users and yield to them all. When the trail forks at **6.9** miles, go right.

The trail drops and crosses an intermittent creek, **7.3** miles. Follow the cairns that mark the route. From here the trail traverses, ducking in and out of several drainages before emerging at the top of an open, knife-edged ridge, **8.2** miles. The trail follows the top of the ridge, descending. You will need to carry your bike down several sets of stairs that begin at **8.5** miles. After negotiating the stairs, continue down the ridge top. At **9** miles, reach a dirt road and turn right. Climb up this gated dirt road toward Windy Ridge Viewpoint. At **10.8** miles, arrive at the viewpoint parking area. From here, turn around and ride back the way you came to complete the Out & Back ride, **21.6** miles.

Gazetteer

Nearby camping: Merrill Lake Campground, Lower Falls Campground
Nearest food, drink, services: Cougar

14 Lewis River

☉☉☉☉

Distance	22.1 miles
Ride	Loop; singletrack, paved road
Duration	3 to 5 hours
Travel time	Portland—2 hours; Seattle—4 hours
Hill factor	A few steep sections, climb on road; 800-foot gain
Skill level	Advanced
Season	Summer, fall
Maps	Green Trails: Lone Butte
Users	Bicyclists, hikers, equestrians
More info	Mount St. Helens National Monument, 360-247-3900

Lewis River crashing over Upper Falls

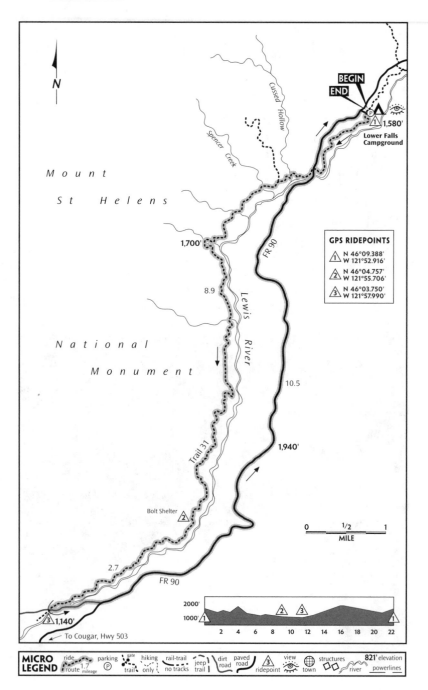

N

BEGIN
END

P
⚠1 1,580'
Lower Falls
Campground

Cussed Hollow

Spencer Creek

Mount

St Helens

1,700'

FR 90

8.9

GPS RIDEPOINTS

⚠1 N 46°09.388'
W 121°52.916'

⚠2 N 46°04.757'
W 121°55.706'

⚠3 N 46°03.750'
W 121°57.990'

Lewis River

National

Monument

10.5

Trail 31

1,940'

Bolt Shelter
⚠2

0   ½   1
MILE

2.7

FR 90

⚠3 1,140'

→ To Cougar, Hwy 503

2000'
1000' ⚠1   ⚠2 ⚠3   ⚠1
2 4 6 8 10 12 14 16 18 20 22

MICRO
LEGEND
ride route · 1.7 mileage · parking Ⓟ · gate · hiking trail only · rail-trail no tracks · jeep trail · dirt road · paved road · ⚠3 ridepoint · view · town · structures · river · 821' elevation powerlines

Prelude

The Lewis River Trail used to be one of the most raved-about trails in Northwest mountain bike lore. That ended in 1996 after several calamitous winter storms washed out numerous sections of trail, the largest being a quarter-mile section taken out by a landslide. Since then the Forest Service has worked, at an agonizingly slow pace, to repair the damage. The work continues, and they claim the trail will be open and ready for riding during the 1998 season. However, much of the trail work remained to be done when I scouted this ride on a wet September day in 1997. Under the current condition, the trail is ridable, with only the landslide difficult to cross; the rest of the blowdown and trail damage are just annoying.

To Get There

From Interstate 5 at Woodland, drive east on State Route 503, also called Lewis River Road. East of the town of Cougar, Lewis River Road becomes Forest Road 90. At the junction of FR 90 and FR 25, start your odometer and bear right, continuing east on FR 90. Pass FR 51, Curly Creek Road, on the right at 5.6 miles. After crossing Lewis River, find Lower Falls Campground on the right at 14.8 miles. Park here.

The Ride

From the junction of FR 90 and the entrance road to Lower Falls Campground, ride toward the campground. Almost immediately, Lewis River Trail 31 crosses the road. Turn right onto the trail and head around the back of the campground, downriver. Reach a T at **0.2** mile and turn right. Pedal down the wide, heavily used trail through old growth and fern. Ride carefully: In a few spots the trail meanders alongside a vertical embankment.

At **1.4** miles, reach FR 90. Turn right, ride a few pedal strokes, then turn left onto the trail again. In past years, a sign at this point has warned that the trail is closed due to washouts. The Forest Service claims that trail repairs will be complete by summer 1998. (Even with the washouts, the trail is ridable, but expect some rugged hike-a-bike sections.) From the road, the trail climbs and descends quickly and unpredictably. At **1.8** miles, cross a bridge over Cussed Hollow Creek. After a short but strenuous climb, **2.1** miles, reach a fork and bear left. Descend and then climb again to a point above a dangerous ravine at **4** miles. **WHOA!** The trail and slope are tilted toward the cliff, so use extreme caution rounding the corner and crossing the creek. Drop back down toward Lewis River.

On the map the next four miles look great—gradual descent along the river. But small slides, washouts, and general lack of maintenance make this a hike-a-bike section, though much of it is ridable. Expect less walking and more excellent riding as the Forest Service reconstructs the trail. At **7.8** miles, a huge landslide of trees and mud blocks the route. With your bike on your shoulder, follow the flagging through the maze. Drop down alongside the river, and at **8.9** miles pass Bolt Shelter on the right. From here the trail winds quickly through thick old growth. This is a fast, as well as popular, section of trail, so keep your speed down.

At **11.6** miles, reach a dirt road and turn left. The road, FR 9039, immediately crosses Lewis River and begins ascending. At **12.4** miles, FR 9039 intersects with FR 90: Turn left onto the paved road. After a short descent, begin a steady climb. **WHOA!** This road has no shoulder and can have heavy traffic on summer weekends. Crest the high point at **15.8** miles, and coast back down toward the river. Cross a bridge over Lewis River at **20.9** miles. Continue up the road to Lower Falls Campground on the right, **22.1** miles, to complete the loop.

Gazetteer

Nearby camping: Lower Falls Campground
Nearest food, drink, services: Eagle Cliff, Cougar

15
LEWIS RIVER
Cussed Hollow
✿✿✿✿

Distance	15.1 miles
Ride	Loop; singletrack, dirt road
Duration	2 to 4 hours
Travel time	Portland—2 hours; Seattle—4 hours
Hill factor	Difficult singletrack climb, hike-a-bike, walking; 2,060-foot gain
Skill level	Advanced
Season	Summer, fall
Maps	Green Trails: Lone Butte
Users	Bicyclists, hikers, equestrians
More info	Mount St. Helens National Monument, 360-247-3900

Cutting a traverse down Trail 19 near Cussed Hollow Creek

Prelude

With a 600-foot-per-mile elevation gain, Wright Meadows Trail certainly qualifies as a hill climber's dream. Most riders—even lean hill climbers on twenty-pound bikes—will have to hike-a-bike at least some of the first four miles, but the dark, lush forest and sweet meadow up on top mitigate the rigors of the difficult ascent. And I haven't even mentioned the fast, romping

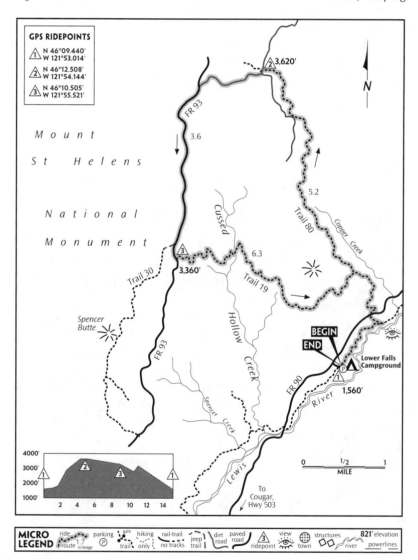

GPS RIDEPOINTS

1. N 46°09.440'
   W 121°53.014'
2. N 46°12.508'
   W 121°54.144'
3. N 46°10.505'
   W 121°55.521'

3,620'

Mount

St Helens

National

Monument

FR 93

3.6

Cussed

Trail 80

Copper Creek

5.2

Trail 30

6.3

3,360'

Trail 19

Spencer
Butte

FR 93

Hollow Creek

BEGIN
END

Lower Falls
Campground

1,560'

FR 90

River

Spencer Creek

Lewis

To
Cougar,
Hwy 503

4000'
3000'
2000'
1000'

2 4 6 8 10 12 14

0   1/2   1
MILE

MICRO LEGEND ride route 1.7 mileage | parking ℗ | gate hiking trail | trail only | rail-trail no tracks | jeep trail | dirt road | paved road | ridepoint | view | town | structures | river | 821' elevation | powerlines descent down Cussed Hollow. During the late afternoon on the day I rode this loop, a large herd of elk milled around in the forest above Copper Creek. So many elk ran across the trail in front of me as I pedaled that I went from admiring theses great animals to wondering what a four-pointed goring wound would look like. Thankfully, I didn't find out.

To Get There

From Interstate 5 at Woodland, drive east on State Route 503, also called Lewis River Road. East of the town of Cougar, Lewis River Road becomes Forest Road 90. At the junction of FR 90 and FR 25, start your odometer and bear right, continuing east on FR 90. Pass FR 51, Curly Creek Road, on the right at 5.6 miles. After crossing Lewis River, find Lower Falls Campground on the right at 14.8 miles. Park here.

The Ride

From the junction of FR 90 and the entrance road to Lower Falls Campground, ride toward the campground. Almost immediately, Lewis River Trail 31 crosses the road: Turn left and ride up the trail. The trail winds around the back of the upper campground loop, then noodles along the high, steep bank above the river. Remember the old mountain bike adage: Don't look where you don't want to go. Reach a fork at **1** mile, and turn back to the left.

After a short climb, cross a paved road and find the start of Wright Meadows Trail, **1.1** miles. Immediately, a series of steep switchbacks provide a preview of this ride—a very steep trail through a deep, beautiful forest. The trail occasionally levels, then heads up again at a truly grueling rate; much of the next three miles may be hike-a-bike. At **1.9** miles, reach a fork and stay to the right. After the **4**-mile mark, the trail levels somewhat. At **4.3** miles, the trail kisses a dirt road that runs parallel on the left: Stay on the trail. From here, the trail noodles through a high meadow. Ignore a spur on the left at **4.9** miles.

At **5.2** miles, reach a dirt road. Turn left on the road, ride to a T, and then turn right, descending down FR 93. Arrive at a fork, **6.2** miles, and turn left, continuing down FR 93, which is now paved. The road undulates, though gradually descends. Pass several lesser spur roads on either side of the main road. At **8.6** miles, pass Spencer Butte Trail on the right. At **8.8** miles, find Cussed Hollow Trail 19, on the left—take this trail.

The trail traverses quickly away from the road, then drops down a series of steep switchbacks. At **10.4** miles, ford Cussed Hollow Creek. The trail cuts a steep traverse away from the creek—so steep, in fact, that you should plan to walk most of the next one-half mile. A rough trail through a clearcut makes the way doubly difficult. Attain the crest of the traverse at **10.9** miles. From here, the trail drops steadily. Watch out for other trail users on this fun section. At **13.2** miles, arrive at a T. Turn right onto Wright Meadows Trail. Cross FR 99 to the trail on the opposite side, **14** miles; then turn back to the right at **14.1** miles. Pedal easily back to Lower Falls Campground to complete the loop, **15.1** miles.

Option

To add about six miles to this loop, take Spencer Butte Trail on the right at the 8.6-mile mark. When the trail ends at FR 93, turn left and ride up to Cussed Hollow Trail, on the right.

Gazetteer

Nearby camping: Lower Falls Campground
Nearest food, drink, services: Eagle Cliff, Cougar

16 LEWIS RIVER
Lone Butte
⚙⚙

Distance	12 miles
Ride	Loop; gated dirt road, dirt road; views
Duration	1 to 2 hours
Travel time	Portland—1.5 hours; Seattle—4.5 hours
Hill factor	Several healthy climbs; 640-foot gain
Skill level	Beginner
Season	Summer, fall
Maps	U.S. Forest Service: Wind River Ranger District
Users	Bicyclists, equestrians
More info	Gifford Pinchot National Forest, Mount Adams District, 509-395-3400

Another road available for exploring, with Mount St. Helens beyond

Prelude

This easy dirt-road ride circumnavigates Lone Butte, a large, cone-shaped mountain that remains visible for much of the ride. Some of the dirt roads are gated, some are not. Ride carefully on the trafficked roads. In addition to this basic loop, lots of exploration is possible in the area: Immediately to the west of Lone Butte Meadows, dirt roads crisscross Crazy Hills; to the north, Squaw Butte Trail angles toward Mosquito Lakes. Both Crazy Hills and Squaw Butte make for much longer and more challenging routes.

To Get There

From Interstate 5 at Woodland, drive east on State Route 503, also called Lewis River Road. East of the town of Cougar, Lewis River Road becomes Forest Road 90. At the junction of FR 90 and FR 25, start your odometer and bear right, continuing east on FR 90. At 5.6 miles, turn right on FR 51, Curly Creek Road. At a T, 13.1 miles, turn left on FR 30, Wind River Road. At 15.3 miles, where FR 30 continues east, take the left fork to stay on Wind River Road. Immediately turn left again into the paved Sno-Park parking area.

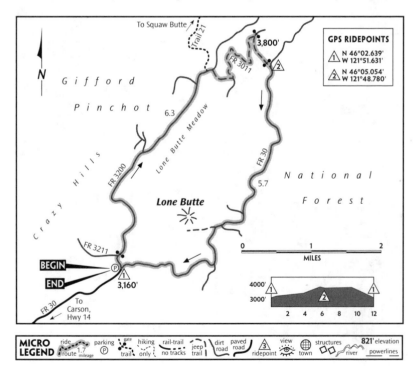

(Alternate route: From SR 14 along the Columbia River near Carson, take FR 30, Wind River Road, north for about 30 miles to Meadow Creek Road.)

The Ride

From the parking area, ride up Meadow Creek Road. At **0.2** mile, reach a fork and go right on gated FR 3200. The gravelly road climbs for about one-half mile, then levels, affording views of Mount Adams. At **2.2** miles, reach a fork: Turn right. Turn right again at the next fork, **3.6** miles. Pass Squaw Butte Trail on the left at **3.8** miles. A few spins farther, arrive at a fork—bear right and begin climbing. The road, smooth in places, rutted in others, climbs steadily. Turn left at a fork at **4.3** miles. At **5.7** miles and with most of the climbing complete, reach a fork and bear right.

At **6.3** miles, pass through a gate and reach FR 30. Turn right and pedal down this road. Watch for vehicle traffic. Stay on the main road, passing numerous spur roads. After **10** miles, the road drops at a quick rate. At **11.9** miles, take the right fork on Meadow Creek Road. Almost immediately, turn left into the parking area to complete the loop, **12** miles.

Gazetteer

Nearby camping: Lower Falls Campground, Paradise Creek Campground
Nearest food, drink, services: Eagle Cliff, Cougar, Wind River

17 Oldman Pass

❀❀❀

Distance	11.9 miles
Ride	Loop; dirt road, doubletrack, singletrack
Duration	1 to 3 hours
Travel time	Portland—1.5 hours; Seattle—4.5 hours
Hill factor	Easy rolling climbs; 340-foot gain
Skill level	Intermediate
Season	Summer, fall
Maps	U.S. Forest Service: Wind River Ranger District
Users	Bicyclists, equestrians
More info	Gifford Pinchot National Forest, Wind River District, 509-427-3200

A foggy day on Forest Road 3054

Prelude

This relatively short, simple ride, located at the northern edge of the Gifford Pinchot National Forest's Wind River Ranger District, features a series of dirt roads and the summertime use of several cross-country ski trails. The dirt-road riding and small elevation gain of this loop nearly qualify it as a two-wheeler, but the trails are rough and not compact because they are used infrequently. This ride functions as an introduction to the roads and trails that crisscross the area—go and explore.

To Get There

From Interstate 5 at Woodland, drive east on State Route 503, also called Lewis River Road. East of the town of Cougar, Lewis River Road becomes Forest Road 90. At the junction of FR 90 and FR 25, start your odometer and bear right, continuing east on FR 90. At 5.6 miles, turn right on FR 51, Curly Creek Road. At a T, 13.1 miles, turn right on FR 30, Wind River Road. At 16 miles, park at the Oldman Pass Sno-Park on the right. (Alternate route: From SR 14 along the Columbia River near Carson, take FR 30, Wind River Road,

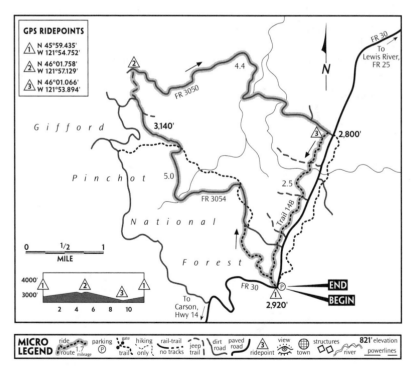

north for about 25 miles; eventually it becomes Wind River Road; continue to Oldman Pass Sno-Park.)

The Ride

From the kiosk on the west side of FR 30, take Snow Foot Trail 148. Follow the blue diamonds on the trees along an ancient doubletrack. At **0.5** mile, reach FR 3054 and turn left, following signs for Scenic Loop. At **1.6** miles, pass a faint trail on the right. Continue along FR 3054, which rises and falls. Pass FR 134 on the right at **4** miles. At **4.6** miles, turn right, leaving the main road to follow signs for Hardtime Loop. **WHOA!** This turn looks more like a big pile of sticks than a trail, and is thus quite easy to miss. Continue pursuing the blue diamonds, and ride down the rough doubletrack.

At **5** miles, arrive at a T with a dirt road. Turn right onto FR 3050. Stay on the main road, ignoring several roads on the left. Finally, **9.4** miles, just before reaching FR 30, turn right onto Snow Foot Trail 148. Primarily a cross-country ski route in winter, this trail gets limited summer use, so the tread is sometimes ridable, sometimes rough, and sometimes nonexistent. Be ready for some technical sections of trail. (If the trail is too rough or overgrown, turn left on one of the numerous dirt roads that cross the trail, ride to FR 30, turn right, and ride back to the parking area at Oldman Pass.) Stay on Snow Foot Trail 148, crossing numerous dirt roads as you gradually climb toward the pass. At **11.7** miles, bear to the left. Reach the parking area at **11.9** miles to complete the loop.

Gazetteer

Nearby camping: Lower Falls Campground, Paradise Creek Campground
Nearest food, drink, services: Eagle Cliff, Cougar, Wind River

YACOLT BURN STATE FOREST
18 Tarbell Trail

✿✿✿✿

Distance	21.7 miles
Ride	Loop; singletrack, dirt road
Duration	3 to 5 hours
Travel time	Portland—1 hour; Seattle—3 hours
Hill factor	Long dirt-road climb, singletrack switchback ascents; 2,020-foot gain
Skill level	Intermediate
Season	Late spring, summer, fall
Maps	Washington State DNR: Yacolt Burn State Forest
Users	Bicyclists, equestrians, hikers
More info	Washington State DNR, Southwest Region, 360-577-2025

Enjoying Hidden Falls from a bridge over Coyote Creek

Prelude

The trails in many DNR-managed Washington State Forests are muddy, inadequately maintained, or overrun by motorcycles. This version of the Tarbell Trail (I eliminated the muddy lowland section) suffers from none of these problems: Most of the trail is in excellent shape and it's off-limits to motorized use. The numerous climbs and extended distance make this a four-wheeler;

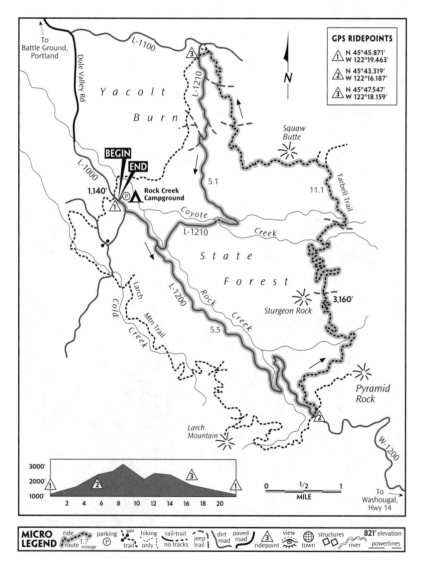

the zippy traverses and fast switchbacks will keep a smile on your face. On the crisp September day I cycled this road-to-trail-to-road loop, I met a couple of riders from Vancouver. They were the only trail users I saw that day.

To Get There

Just east of Vancouver, Washington, from the junction of Interstate 205 and State Route 500, take SR 500 east. Drive just over 1 mile and bear north on SR 503. Take SR 503 about 5 miles north of Battle Ground. Turn right on Northeast Rock Creek Road and zero your odometer. Stay on the main road, which, after several name changes, becomes Northeast Lucia Falls Road. At 8.8 miles, turn right on Northeast Sunset Falls Road. At 11.2 miles, turn right on Northeast Dole Valley Road. Stay on the main road, which turns to dirt when it becomes Road L-1000. At 16.1 miles, find Rock Creek Campground on the left.

The Ride

From the junction of Road L-1000 and the entrance to Rock Creek Campground, pedal up gravelly L-1000. At **0.2** mile, take the left fork onto L-1200 and descend for a short distance. Before long, though, the climb begins. Stay on the main road, ignoring numerous lesser spurs as you ride through recent

The traverse toward Pyramid Rock on Tarbell Trail

clearcuts. The road, rough in a few sections, continues up. After several long switchbacks, the road levels and becomes quite wide as it bears to the left. At this wide, level spot, **5.5** miles, find Tarbell Trail on the left: Take this trail.

After a short, steep, rocky section, reach a fork, **5.6** miles, and bear left. From here the well-maintained trail traverses toward Pyramid Rock, which juts up from the ridgeline ahead. Cross a bridge at **7.3** miles. Rock Creek flows over a number of large rocks, forming a small falls at this point. The trail switchbacks up the side of a ridge, affording more views of Pyramid Rock. Crest the top of the ridge at **8.6** miles. Almost immediately, the trail crosses an old jeep track—go straight across. Glide down a long series of switchbacks. At **10.6** miles, the trail again crosses an old road. Drop again, but as you cross Coyote Creek at **10.8** miles, stop for a moment to soak in Hidden Falls, which plummets from high above just upstream.

From the falls, begin climbing again. At a fork, **12.5** miles, go left toward Tarbell Picnic Area. Descending, pass a lesser trail on the right at **13** miles. Over the next mile, the forest opens as the trail winds upward to cross another ridge. After passing over a wide ridge, the trail crosses three jeep trails, one at **14** miles, a second at **14.3** miles, and a third at **15.6** miles. At each crossing, continue straight ahead on the trail. When the trail forks at **16.3** miles, bear left toward Rock Creek Campground. At **16.6** miles, reach a dirt road, L-1210, and turn left onto the road. (The trail continues to Rock Creek Campground, but for most of the year this next section is extremely muddy and heavily used by equestrians.)

Stay on the main road, L-1210, as you descend quickly. Take the right fork at **16.8** miles and again at **17.8** miles. At **18.3** miles, take the left fork. At **18.6** miles, ignore a lesser road on the right. Cross Coyote Creek at **19.3** miles. At **19.6** miles, you'll find that the south fork of Coyote Creek did a fine job of washing the bridge away. Take the faint trail around to the right and ford the creek. Continue down the road. Ignore a road back on the left at **20.1** miles. Reach the junction of L-1210 and L-1200 at **20.8** miles. Turn right onto L-1200, riding toward Rock Creek Campground. At **21.5** miles, reach a fork and turn right. Spin down to the entrance of the campground to complete the loop, **21.7** miles.

Gazetteer

Nearby camping: Rock Creek Campground
Nearest food, drink, services: Battle Ground, Yacolt

19

Larch Mountain

⊕⊕⊕⊕

Distance	13.7 miles
Ride	Loop; singletrack, dirt road; views
Duration	2 to 5 hours
Travel time	Portland—1 hour; Seattle—3 hours
Hill factor	Tough dirt-road and singletrack climb, 2-mile hike-a-bike; 2,300-foot gain
Skill level	Expert
Season	Late spring, summer, fall
Maps	Washington State DNR: Yacolt Burn State Forest
Users	Bicyclists, equestrians, hikers
More info	Washington State DNR, Southwest Region, 360-577-2025

A clearcut on the slopes of Rock Creek

Prelude

I scouted this trail, for the first time, in the late afternoon on a day that wasn't supposed to be quite so cold and rainy; during the descent, I mentally purchased a lot of cold-weather riding gear. After a long dirt-road climb, plan on a two-mile hike-a-bike to reach the top of the ride, slightly more if you want to bag Larch Mountain. Large rocks and loose soil, kicked up by motor-

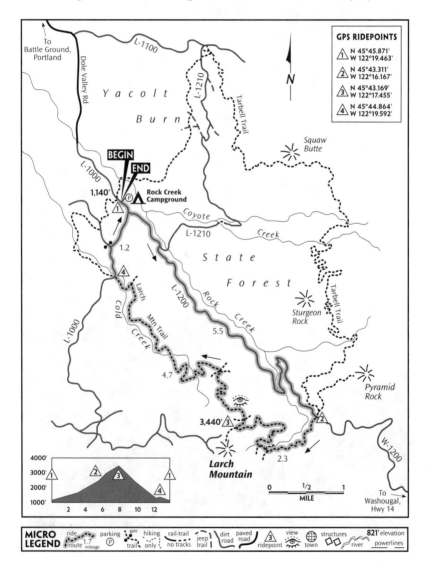

GPS RIDEPOINTS
1. N 45°45.871' W 122°19.463'
2. N 45°43.311' W 122°16.167'
3. N 45°43.169' W 122°17.455'
4. N 45°44.864' W 122°19.592'

To Battle Ground, Portland

Dole Valley Rd

L-1100

L-1210

Tarbell Trail

Yacolt

Burn

Squaw Butte

N

BEGIN
END

L-1000

1,140'

Rock Creek Campground

Coyote

Creek

L-1210

State

Forest

1.2

Larch

Cold Creek

L-1000

Mtn Trail

L-1200

Rock

Creek

5.5

Sturgeon Rock

Tarbell Trail

4.7

Pyramid Rock

3,440'

Larch Mountain

2.3

W-1200

0   1/2   1
MILE

To Washougal, Hwy 14

4000'
3000'
2000'
1000'
2 4 6 8 10 12

MICRO LEGEND — ride route 1.7 mileage — parking P — gate — hiking trail only — rail-trail no tracks — jeep trail — dirt road — paved road — 3 ridepoint — view — town — structures — river — 821' elevation — powerlines

cyclists poaching this trail, make the climb difficult; but strong, skilled, and determined riders should be able to ride much of it. The descent is technical but fast and fun. Check your brakes at the top.

To Get There

Just east of Vancouver, Washington, from the junction of Interstate 205 and State Route 500, take SR 500 east. Drive just over 1 mile and bear north on SR 503. Take SR 503 about 5 miles north of Battle Ground. Turn right on Northeast Rock Creek Road and start your odometer here. Stay on the main road, which, after several name changes, becomes Northeast Lucia Falls Road. At 8.8 miles, turn right on Northeast Sunset Falls Road. At 11.2 miles, turn right on Northeast Dole Valley Road. Stay on the main road, which turns to dirt when it becomes Road L-1000. At 16.1 miles, find Rock Creek Campground on the left.

The Ride

From the junction of Road L-1000 and the entrance to Rock Creek Campground, pedal up gravelly L-1000. At **0.2** mile, take the left fork onto L-1200 and descend for a short distance. Before long, though, the climb begins. Stay on the main road, ignoring numerous lesser spurs as you ride through recent clearcuts. The road, rough in a few sections, continues up. After a several long switchbacks, the road levels and becomes quite wide as it bears to the left. At this wide, level spot, **5.5** miles, find Larch Trail on the right.

Wide, rocky, and steep, Larch Mountain Trail climbs

A warm day on Larch Mountain Trail

vigorously away from L-1200. The large, loose rocks make the riding difficult and at times frustrating, a probable two-mile hike-a-bike. At a fork, **6.4** miles, bear right. After a few pedal strokes, ignore a wide trail back to the right. At **6.5** miles, reach another fork and go right. Cross Grouse Creek and continue the tough ascent up an open ridge. On a clear day the ridge offers views of Mount Adams. At **7.8** miles, reach a fork that denotes the ride's high point. Take a hard right and ride toward Cold Creek Campground (the left fork climbs to the top of Larch Mountain).

At **7.9** miles, pass straight through a four-way intersection. The trail, quite technical here, traverses downward across an open, rocky slope, exposing more volcano views to the north. Below on the right at **8.4** miles, pass a solitary picnic table on the edge of the scree hillside. It must have been placed there by mountain bikers who wanted a rest stop prior to the fast, steep, root-strewn descent. From here the trail drops into the forest and corkscrews down the northern flank of Larch Mountain. At **9.7** miles, reach a confusing five-way intersection: Go straight through, ignoring two trails on the right and one wide trail on the left.

After several more fast switchbacks, cross a bridge over Cold Creek. Cross the creek two more times then, at **11.1** miles, ignore two lesser trails in succession on the right. The trail crosses the creek again, then rolls and swells to a road, L-1000, at **12.5** miles. Turn right on L-1000 (the trail continues, but the next two miles are often extremely muddy and heavily used by equestrians). When the road forks at **12.9** miles, bear right. The road forks again at **13.5** miles: This time bear left toward Rock Creek Campground. Reach the entrance to the campground at **13.7** miles to complete the loop.

Gazetteer

Nearby camping: Rock Creek Campground
Nearest food, drink, services: Battle Ground, Yacolt

YACOLT BURN STATE FOREST

20 Three Corner Rock

☼☼☼

Distance	17.4 miles
Ride	Loop; singletrack, dirt road
Duration	2 to 5 hours
Travel time	Portland—45 minutes; Seattle—3.5 hours
Hill factor	Long, sometimes steep, climbs, some hike-a-bike; 1,660-foot gain
Skill level	Intermediate
Season	Late spring, summer, fall
Maps	Washington State DNR: Yacolt Burn State Forest
Users	Bicyclists, equestrians, hikers
More info	Washington State DNR, Southwest Region, 360-577-2025

Prelude

I rode the last mile of Three Corner Rock Trail with the help of a flashlight. I didn't plan it that way, but for me this loop turned into an unpredictable chameleon that climbed when I thought it should descend and switchbacked down toward the creek when I thought a prudent trail would certainly aim

Bridge over Stebbins Creek

high for the top of the ridge. I like it when a trail surprises me, taking me over a bridge, across a slope, down into an unexpected part of the forest. It's just too bad that the sun is so darned predictable, always getting dark exactly when it's supposed to. Despite the surprising twists and turns, the trail is in good shape and ridable most of the way—a difficult but exhilarating three-wheeler.

To Get There

From Interstate 205 east of Vancouver, Washington, take State Route 14 eastbound. Drive about 10 miles, then take a left on 15th Street and drive into the town of Washougal. Zero your odometer here. Proceed about 0.25 mile and pass straight through the stoplight; 15th Street becomes 17th Street and finally becomes Washougal River Road. Stay on Washougal River Road. At

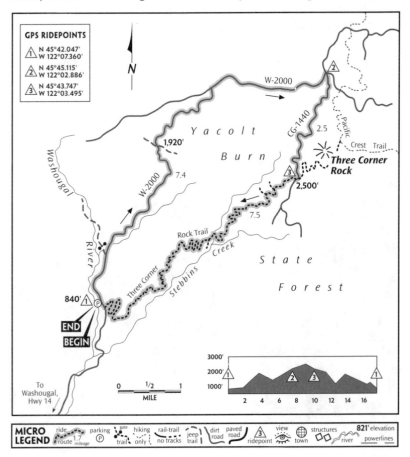

18.5 miles, cross Washougal River and take the right fork onto a gravel road. This becomes Road W-2000. At 22.1 miles, reach Three Corner Rock Trailhead on the left.

The Ride

From Three Corner Rock Trailhead on Road W-2000, pedal easily up the road, which parallels Washougal River. Around the **1**-mile point, ignore a gated road on the left; follow the main road as it bends to the right away from Washougal River. At **1.7** miles, after a few gentle ups and downs, the road begins a serious ascent toward Deer Creek Divide. At **3.5** miles, reach the top of the divide at a four-way intersection: Go straight, continuing on Road 2000. The road descends rapidly.

Just after crossing Deer Creek, **5.2** miles, take the right fork toward Three Corner Rock. Road 2000 climbs steadily, following the creek and offering occasional glimpses of the Rock. When the road forks at **7.4** miles, turn right on Road CG-1440. The road descends for a short pitch, crosses a creek, then climbs again to a saddle at **8.9** miles. Descend to the **9.9**-mile mark, and find Three Corner Rock Trail, which crosses the road here. Turn right on the trail.

The trail quickly zips into the woods, then rises and falls as it descends a ridge. At **10.3** miles, pass a trail on the right that heads toward a viewpoint. When the trail forks again at **10.6** miles, go left. At **11.4** miles, the trail begins a series of steep switchbacks down toward Stebbins Creek. Walk across an extremely narrow, somewhat tilted, all-and-all sketchy wood bridge over the creek at **12.5** miles and immediately begin climbing. Ignore the horse by-pass trail on the left, and continue grinding and switchbacking up the steep trail. Ride over a high point (one of many on this ride) at the **13.6**-mile mark.

After a traverse, cut another series of ragged switchbacks down toward the creek; it's difficult to figure out exactly where the trail is heading. Finally, the trail traces a steep traverse up the ridge between Stebbins Creek and Washougal River. Ride over the top of the ridge at **16.3** miles. From here the trail switchbacks down toward the Washougal River. At **17.1** miles, turn left on a jeep trail. At **17.2** miles, reach a T at Road W-2000 and turn right. Ride north on W-2000, and find Three Corner Rock Trailhead on the left at **17.4** miles to complete the loop.

Gazetteer

Nearby camping: Beacon Rock State Park Campground
Nearest food, drink, services: Washougal

21 Nestor Peak

✹✹✹

Distance	9.8 miles
Ride	Loop; singletrack, dirt road; views
Duration	1 to 3 hours
Travel time	Portland—1.5 hours; Seattle—4.5 hours
Hill factor	Steep climbs, some hike-a-bike; 1,620-foot gain
Skill level	Advanced
Season	Late spring, summer, fall
Maps	Washington State DNR: Buck Creek Trail System; Green Trails: Willard
Users	Bicyclists, equestrians, hikers
More info	Washington State DNR, Southeast Region, 509-925-8510

Prelude

Both the DNR and Green Trails maps show a series of trails that circle the entire Buck Creek Basin, a twenty-five- to thirty-mile loop. Unfortunately, large sections of that loop have not been maintained in several years, thus full armor and fourteen hours of daylight are recommended. The DNR

Zipping down the trail from Nestor Peak

should do a better job of keeping these trails maintained. In addition, neither map listed above notes all of the dirt roads and trails that exist in the area. This means that the exploration potential is high, but watch out for the radically steep topography. This Nestor Peak route, which travels some of the trails of the larger Buck Creek loop, consists of a dirt-road climb and fast singletrack descent.

To Get There

Drive about 63 miles east of Vancouver, Washington, on State Route 14. Before White Salmon, turn left on Alternate SR 141 and zero your odometer. At 2.3 miles, turn left on SR 141 northbound. At 4.3 miles, turn left on Northwestern Lake Road. Soon after crossing the White Salmon River, the road

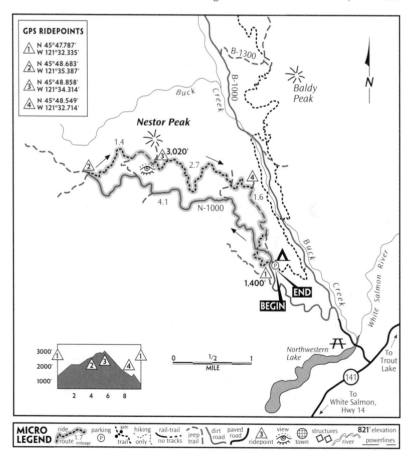

turns to gravel. At 5.7 miles, take the left fork onto Road N-1000. At 7.2 miles, take the right fork, staying on N-1000. At 7.7 miles, turn right and park at Trailhead 1.

The Ride

From the junction of N-1000 and the short road that leads to Trailhead 1, ride up N-1000. Reach a fork at **0.2** mile and bear left. The road climbs at a steep grade. At **0.4** mile, pass a trail that crosses the road—continue up the road. At a fork, **1.3** miles, go left, staying on N-1000. At **1.6** miles, the road wraps around the south side of Nestor Peak, traversing through a dry fir and oak forest. Reach a fork at **2.6** miles: Bear right and begin climbing again. At the next fork, just past the **3**-mile mark, bear left.

At **4.1** miles, arrive at the junction of N-1000 and N-1700. **WHOA!** Turn right onto a faint trail that climbs east toward Nestor Peak. The next mile—steep, unmaintained, sometimes rocky—will be a hike-a-bike for many riders. Using your sixth sense (route finding) to follow the faint path, bear to the left at **4.6** miles. After a few more twists and climbs, drop down a narrow, brushy chute to a road, **5.3** miles. Turn left and ride up the road. At **5.5** miles, find the marked but faint trail on the right (the road continues a short distance up to the top of Nestor Peak).

Before making the turn onto the trail, enjoy the views to the south of Mount Hood and the rolling hills of north-central Oregon. From the road, follow the singletrack as it drops quickly and paints a big fat smile on your face. **WHOA!** Beware of the high endo potential and watch out for other trail users. At **7.5** miles, bear right onto a doubletrack. Almost immediately, take a trail on the left. After another nice section of singletrack, bear right on a second doubletrack, **8.2** miles, and make a fast traverse. At **9** miles, find a trail on the right marked only by white diamonds. Take this trail and begin a short, difficult climb. The trail crosses a road at **9.1** miles. From here the trail roller-coasters, then finally drops to the junction of N-1000 and the short road to Trailhead 1 to complete the loop, **9.8** miles.

Gazetteer

Nearby camping: Moss Creek Campground, Beacon Rock State Park
Nearest food, drink, services: White Salmon

COLUMBIA RIVER GORGE

22 Buck Creek

✿✿✿

Distance	11.7 miles
Ride	Loop; singletrack, dirt road
Duration	1 to 3 hours
Travel time	Portland—1.5 hours; Seattle—4.5 hours
Hill factor	Difficult, steep climbs; 1,800-foot gain
Skill level	Advanced
Season	Late spring, summer, fall
Maps	Washington State DNR: Buck Creek Trail System
Users	Bicyclists, equestrians, hikers
More info	Washington State DNR, Southeast Region, 509-925-8510

A break in the steep descent from Baldy Peak

Prelude

Though this loop is short and the elevation gain is under 2,000 feet, parts of the climb seem vertical, and, for balance I suppose, a few short sections of the descent seem vertical as well. Short sections of the singletrack are perfect. Watch for vehicles on the road and other users on the trail, especially equestrians. Strong riders may want to combine this ride with Ride 21, Nestor Peak, for a full day of riding.

To Get There

Drive about 63 miles east of Vancouver, Washington, on State Route 14. Before White Salmon, turn left on Alternate SR 141 and zero your odometer. At 2.3 miles, turn left on SR 141 northbound. At 4.3 miles, turn left on North-

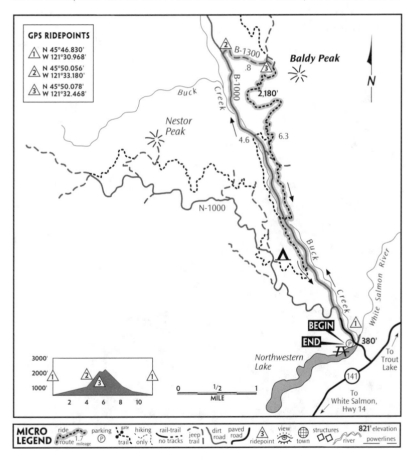

western Lake Road. Cross the White Salmon River and immediately turn left into the parking area at Northwestern Lake Park.

The Ride

From the parking area, ride away from the river on Nestor Peak Road. At **0.2** mile, the road becomes gravel. At a fork, **0.6** mile, bear right on Road B-1000 toward Buck Creek Trailhead 2. Continue up the road, passing several trails along the way. At **4** miles, the road bends to the right and begins a serious climb. The steep grade and gravelly roadbed make the climb a frustrating grind. When the road forks at **4.6** miles, turn right. Though this dirt road, B-1300, provides better traction, the grade is much steeper, and for the next mile you will lament the fact that you didn't buy a far bigger cog for your rear freewheel.

Just before the top of the hill, the road forks, **5.4** miles: Take the lesser road to the right. This road becomes a doubletrack, then quickly a single-track, as it negotiates the rugged, hectic western slope of Baldy Peak. The trail mellows and traverses. Reach a fork at **8.1** miles—bear left. When the trail meets a dirt road at **8.2** miles, bear left. At **8.3** miles, take the singletrack, which exits the road on the right. At the next fork, **9.3** miles, turn back to the right, following the trail signs.

At **9.5** miles, the trail crosses Road B-1000. Ride up the trail on the opposite side of the road. After a few pedal strokes, reach a T—turn left. Ignore a trail on the left at **9.6** miles and another on the right at **10.2** miles. WHOA! At **10.3** miles, turn back to the left on an unmarked, easy-to-miss trail. Reach B-1000 after two quick turns: Turn right. Stay on the main road as you ride south on B-1000. Complete the ride upon reaching Northwestern Lake Park on the right at **11.7** miles.

Gazetteer

Nearby camping: Moss Creek Campground, Beacon Rock State Park
Nearest food, drink, services: White Salmon

23 Elochoman State Forest

⚙⚙⚙

Distance	7.3 miles
Ride	Loop; singletrack, doubletrack
Duration	1 to 2 hours
Travel time	Portland—2 hours; Seattle—3 hours
Hill factor	Rolling, some steep sections; 140-foot gain
Skill level	Advanced
Season	Year-round
Maps	Washington State DNR: Elochoman Area
Users	Bicyclists, hikers, equestrians, motorcyclists
More info	Washington State DNR, Southwest Region, 360-577-2025

Rolling through Elochoman State Forest

Prelude

I'm not sure it has ever rained on me with more intensity than on the day I rode Bradley Bike Trail at Elochoman State Forest: The deep puddles nearly swallowed me; the slick roots proved treacherous. If you are in the mood to get really, really muddy, this is the ride for you. This short loop, primarily used by motorized users, is a good starting point for explorations into the wet, fertile, tree-growing lands near Elochoman River. While this is the only trail noted on the DNR map of the area, many other trails and barricaded dirt roads exist.

To Get There

Drive about 29 miles west of Longview on State Route 4. Turn right on Elochoman Valley Road and start your odometer here. At 3.8 miles, turn right on Beaver Creek Road. At 8.4 miles, turn left on Road B-1000. At 10.3 miles, reach Bradley Bike Trail and Recreation Area on the right. From the sign, take the next two quick right turns to get into the parking area.

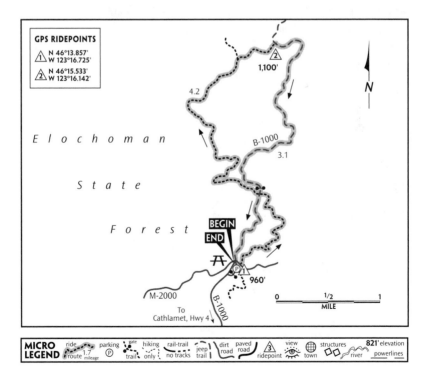

The Ride

From the parking area, trails exit in every direction, so be careful to get on the correct one. Ride to the five-way intersection at the entrance of the parking area and turn right. Almost immediately, find a trail on the left and take it. The wide, muddy, root-strewn trail winds through a thick forest. At **1.3** miles, cross a road and catch the trail on the opposite side. The trail continues the muddy, sometimes technical roller coaster through the woods. Reach a fork at **3.8** miles and turn right, following the trail signs. At **4.2** miles, ignore a trail back on the left.

After a short push up a very steep hill, continue following the trail signs. The trail soon widens to become a narrow road, B-1000. Stay on the main road. At **6.4** miles, steer around several cement barriers and continue down the road. The road crosses the trail, **6.5** miles, but keep riding south on B-1000. At **7.2** miles, reach the junction of B-1000 and M-2000. Turn left and ride back to the parking area to complete the loop, **7.3** miles.

Gazetteer

Nearby camping: Seaquest State Park, Fort Canby State Park
Nearest food, drink, services: Cathlamet

24 Tapeworm Trail

☉☉☉

Distance	3.8 miles
Ride	Loop; singletrack
Duration	1 to 2 hours
Travel time	Seattle—20 minutes
Hill factor	Constant micro climbs and descents
Skill level	Expert
Season	Year-round
Maps	USGS: Renton
Users	Bicyclists
More info	Send an SASE to CycoActive Products, 701 34th Avenue, Seattle, WA 98122

Prelude

From the scotch broom nests and tangled thickets of a knoll just east of Interstate 405 in Renton (of all places), a great in-city mountain bike trail has emerged. The Tapeworm has become the hot ticket for expert mountain bikers interested in fine-tuning their bike-handling skills. When do you get the opportunity to ride a trail named Tapeworm or Mr. DNA and race past electrical substations and under multiple sets of power lines? Not often enough. With supertight twists and turns, roots, stumps, logs, and tunnels,

Yet one more hairpin turn on the Tapeworm Trail

this expert-level trail equals Skookum Flats' technicality. The signature of the trail—narrow, slow, hairpin turns—will make you feel as though you're a ball in a pinball machine. But like pinball, you have to play by the rules: Don't cut corners or otherwise make the trail easier to ride and don't cross from one switchback to another, or else the magic of the continuous, narrow, one-way trail will be ruined. Many trails exist in this small area, and some of the spur trails have not been mentioned in the ride description below—follow the directions carefully.

To Get There

Take I-405 south to exit 4 in Renton. Off the ramp, merge with Sunset Boulevard North. Turn right on Bronson Way North, cross the bridge, then turn left

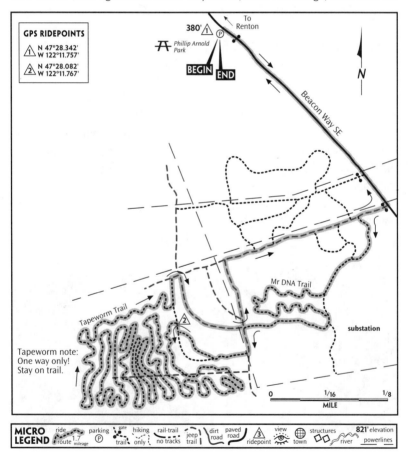

on Mill Avenue South. Go straight through the light, and turn left on Renton Avenue South. After a steep hill, turn left on South Seventh Street, then veer right on Beacon Way South to Philip Arnold Park. Stop at the parking lot adjacent to the baseball diamond.

The Ride

From the paved parking area adjacent to the playfields, ride up Beacon Way through a gate that is usually closed. At the top of the hill, **0.25** mile, meet the first of many sets of power lines. Turn to the right, pass through several concrete barriers, and ride along a narrow dirt road. At **0.3** mile, turn back to the left on a narrow trail. The trail rounds the corner of a substation. Then at **0.4** mile, turn right on a lesser trail into the brush: the beginning of Mr. DNA. After numerous twists and turns, ups and downs, finish the double helix at a T—turn right, **0.8** mile. You have seen your tapeworm future.

At **0.85** mile, take the right fork. The singletrack drops to a four-way intersection at **0.95** mile; go left onto a dirt road. Immediately a singletrack exits to the right—take that trail. The trail drops, bearing to the right. When the trail forks at **1** mile, bear right. At **1.05** miles, find a faint trail on the left and take it. This is the start of the Tapeworm. Remember: Do not cut any of the switchbacks or try to smooth out the route; this is one continuous trail and was built with expert riders in mind. Once you enter, bailing out and bushwhacking home is unacceptable. Right from the start, the trail snakes frantically through the thick brush, coiling and re-coiling, rising and falling. After fourteen charmed switchbacks, the Tapeworm ends at a T at **3.15** miles— turn left. Ride to a four-way intersection and turn right, then immediately turn right again onto a singletrack. At **3.3** miles, reach another four-way intersection and turn left. Bear right at the immediate fork and ride straight to a T at **3.35** miles. Turn right and ride up this dirt road, adjacent to a big set of power lines, to a T at Beacon Way South at **3.55** miles. Turn left and ride back to Philip Arnold Park at **3.8** miles to complete the loop.

Gazetteer

Nearby camping: Renton jail (!)
Nearest food, drink, services: Renton

25 Preston Railroad Trail

⚙⚙⚙⚙

Distance	12 miles
Ride	Loop; singletrack, dirt road
Duration	2 to 4 hours
Travel time	Seattle—40 minutes; Ellensburg—1.5 hours
Hill factor	Tough 3-mile climb to start; 1,230-foot gain
Skill level	Advanced
Season	Spring, summer, fall (closed November 15 to April 15)
Maps	Washington State DNR: Tiger Mountain State Forest
Users	Bicyclists, hikers, equestrians
More info	Washington State DNR, South Puget Sound Region, 360-825-1631

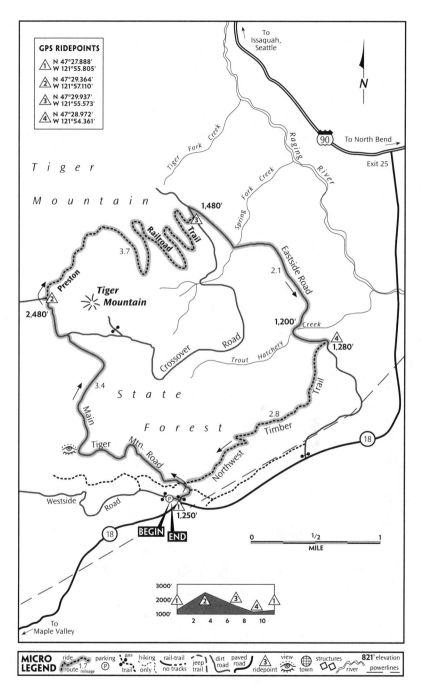

GPS RIDEPOINTS

△1 N 47°27.888'
    W 121°55.805'
△2 N 47°29.364'
    W 121°57.110'
△3 N 47°29.937'
    W 121°55.573'
△4 N 47°28.972'
    W 121°54.361'

To Issaquah, Seattle

N

90 To North Bend

Exit 25

Tiger Fork Creek

Raging River

Spring Fork Creek

Tiger

Mountain

1,480'
△3

Railroad Trail

3.7

Eastside Road

2.1

Preston

△2

Tiger
Mountain

1,200'

Creek

△4
1,280'

2,480'

Crossover Road

Trout Hatchery

3.4

State

Main

Forest

Timber Trail

2.8

Northwest

Tiger Mtn. Road

18

Westside Road

P
△1
1,250'

BEGIN END

18

0   1/2   1
MILE

To Maple Valley

3000'
2000' △1   △2   △3   △4   △1
1000'
      2 4 6 8 10

MICRO LEGEND — ride route 1.7 mileage · parking P · gate hiking trail only · rail-trail no tracks · jeep trail · dirt road paved road · △3 ridepoint · view town · structures · river · 821' elevation powerlines

83

Prelude

For years the Backcountry Bicycle Trails Club (BBTC) has lobbied the Department of Natural Resources to get the Preston Railroad Trail—the most heavily used mountain bike trail in King County—open year-round. Unfortunately, the South Puget Sound Regional office of the DNR has done a terrible job of managing mountain-bike recreation on Tiger Mountain, and legal riding on the trail, between November and April, won't happen anytime soon. Recently, the DNR prevented the BBTC from repairing this woefully unmaintained trail that, in places, looks more like a wild rocky stream than a popular mountain-bike route. And this is after the DNR spent a lot of money helicoptering in gravel so the BBTC could work on the trail. The DNR should open this trail and others on the southeast side of Tiger Mountain to year-round mountain biking. If you think so too, give them a call.

For those unfamiliar with the Preston Railroad Trail: It starts with a steep three-mile dirt-road climb and is followed by a rocky, root-strewn, muddy—extremely jarring yet somehow exhilarating—section of trail that switchbacks down the eastern flank of Tiger Mountain. There are plenty of other trails that I'd rather ride, but if you only have a couple of hours and you want to give your full-suspension bike a good workout, then it's the Preston or bust. Warning: I have heard many reports of cars getting broken into at the Tiger Mountain trailhead.

To Get There

From Seattle, drive east on Interstate 90 to exit 25. Start your odometer here and take State Route 18 south. At 4.5 miles, find a large dirt pullout on the right just after cresting the summit. Turn in here, then take the dirt road on the left, Westside Road, and proceed to the parking area, 4.7 miles.

The Ride

Begin from the parking area one-quarter mile up Westside Road. Ride back down the hill to the dirt pullout near SR 18 and turn left onto a gated dirt road, Main Tiger Mountain Road. Without much warm-up or warning, the road becomes steep, winding up the south side of East Tiger Mountain. Pass both Northwest Timber Trail on the right at **0.4** mile and Connector Trail on the left at **0.5** mile. Continue the brutal climb. At **1.6** miles, the road levels somewhat at a viewpoint. From here you get great views of Mount Rainier as well as the Green, Cedar, and White River valleys. Though the worst of the climbing is now over, the grade continues higher. Arrive at a T, **3** miles, and take a left (the right fork leads to the top of East Tiger in 1.4 miles).

WHOA! At **3.4** miles find Preston Railroad Trail, which exits the road on the right. This turn is easily missed by anyone who has blacked out due to the exhausting climb. Enter a deep forest, winding along a fun, twisting trail. The trail drops and then climbs a bit until it meets what remains of the railroad bed, an old logging railroad grade built in the early 1900s, at **4.1** miles. The railroad grade, straight and evenly sloped compared with the initial section of trail, switchbacks down the west side of Tiger Mountain, descending rapidly on a bumpy and jarring tread. Blowdown, running water, rocks, and roots make some walking inevitable on this difficult section.

At **7.1** miles, reach a road: Take a left, downhill. Ride a short distance to another road at **7.3** miles. This time turn right and traverse, gradually descending. Ignore a road on the right at **8.1** miles. At **9** miles, after a steep final descent, the road bottoms out and then climbs for a short distance. At the top of the hill, **9.2** miles, find Northwest Timber Trail on the right. Take this trail. Roller-coaster along the generally easy grades of this wonderful, though overused, trail. After several bridge crossings, reach Main Tiger Mountain Road at **11.6** miles. Turn left and ride down to a gate. Just past the gate, turn right on Westside Road, and pedal up the gentle grade to the parking area to complete the ride, **12** miles.

Gazetteer

Nearby camping: Tolt-MacDonald Park, dispersed camping in the Middle Fork of the Snoqualmie River valley
Nearest food, drink, services: Issaquah

The wet, rocky Preston Railroad Trail

26 Boxley Creek

Distance	9.8 miles
Ride	Out & Back; rail-trail
Duration	1 hour
Travel time	Seattle—50 minutes; Ellensburg—1.5 hours
Hill factor	Nearly flat; 340-foot gain
Skill level	Beginner
Season	Year-round
Maps	Green Trails: Bandera
Users	Bicyclists, hikers, equestrians
More info	King County Parks, 206-296-4232

The Snoqualmie Valley Trail bends southwest toward Rattlesnake Lake

Prelude

I've ridden this section of the Snoqualmie Valley Trail numerous times. It's a lovely, calming rail-trail ride above Boxley Creek and then along South Fork of the Snoqualmie River. I rode it once in January, the wide, compact trail covered with a light dusting of snow, and I had a wonderful time. This trail, part of the old Milwaukee Railroad, runs from Duvall to Rattlesnake Lake, then over Snoqualmie Pass and across eastern Washington to Idaho. From Rattlesnake Lake eastward, the trail is managed by Washington State Parks and the Washington State Department of Natural Resources. A new trailhead is scheduled to be built in 1998 that may slightly alter the beginning of this ride.

To Get There

From Seattle, drive east on Interstate 90 to exit 32. Start your odometer at the end of the exit ramp, then turn right onto 436th Avenue Southeast. This becomes Cedar Falls Road Southeast. Stay on Cedar Falls Road to Rattlesnake Lake, 3.1 miles. Park in the gravel lots next to the lake. Note: A new parking

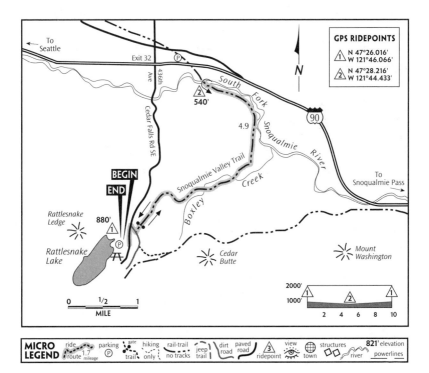

lot and trailhead are planned for this site and may slightly change these directions.

The Ride

From the parking area near Rattlesnake Lake, ride back toward Interstate 90 on Cedar Falls Road. At **0.3** mile, turn right onto a gravel road. Almost immediately, turn left onto the Snoqualmie Valley Trail, a wide, gravel rail-trail. Ever so gradually, the trail descends toward Boxley Creek. Cross a high bridge over the creek-carved canyon below. Continue down the gentle grade. After crossing a second bridge, the trail bends to the left as Boxley Creek merges with South Fork of the Snoqualmie River below on the right. The rail-trail parallels the river. At **4.8** miles, the trail crosses a small residential road. A few pedal strokes farther, reach a bridge over South Fork of the Snoqualmie River, **4.9** miles. This is a good place to turn around. Ride back to Rattlesnake Lake to finish the Out & Back ride, **9.8** miles.

Option

The parking area at Rattlesnake Lake also functions as a trailhead for another easy rail-trail, the John Wayne Pioneer Trail, part of Iron Horse State Park. To explore this trail, go straight on the gravel road at the 0.3-mile mark. At 0.6 mile, take a narrow trail into the woods on the left. At 1 mile, reach John Wayne Pioneer Trail and turn left.

Gazetteer

Nearby camping: Denny Creek Campground
Nearest food, drink, services: North Bend

27 Snoqualmie Tunnel

⊕⊕

Distance	6.4 miles
Ride	Out & Back; wide gravel rail-trail
Duration	1 hour
Travel time	Seattle—1 hour; Ellensburg—1 hour
Hill factor	Flat; 120-foot gain
Skill level	Beginner
Season	Summer (tunnel open May 1 through October 31)
Maps	Mount Baker-Snoqualmie National Forest: North Bend District
Users	Bicyclists, hikers
More info	Washington State Parks, 800-233-0321

Prelude

A ride through the Snoqualmie Tunnel rates as one of those unique experiences that I'd recommend to anyone. Washington State Parks regraded the rail-trail tread and then built a trailhead nearby, making the two-and-a-half-mile-long tunnel not only easy but easily accessible. Riding through the tunnel along the John Wayne Pioneer Trail (part of Iron Horse State Park) is easy and fun, but the darkness cloaks the ride in a mysterious, not-quite-dangerous atmosphere. It's a great destination for cyclists with kids. Just remember to bring a bike light. Warning: The tunnel can be cold even during the summer, so be sure to bring along a wind shell and hat.

To Get There

From Seattle, drive east on Interstate 90 to exit 54, just past Snoqualmie Summit. Zero your odometer at the end of the exit ramp. Turn right, then immediately left, following signs for Iron Horse State Park. At 0.5 mile, turn right, continuing toward Iron Horse State Park. Find Keechelus trailhead on the right at 1 mile.

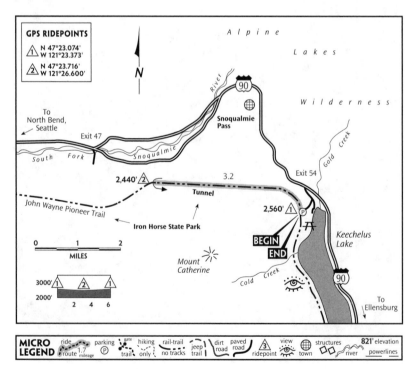

The Ride

Facing the trail from the parking area at Keechelus trailhead, turn right onto the wide, gravel rail-trail, following the signs to the tunnel. At **0.6** mile, pass by a trail kiosk and then through a white gate. Just around the next bend in the trail, reach the entrance to the tunnel, **0.8** mile.

From the tunnel's eastern mouth, you should be able to see a pinpoint of light at the western end of the tunnel, about two and a half miles distant. Turn on your light and ride through the dark, sometimes wet tunnel. Emerge from the darkness at the opposite end, **3.2** miles. Retrace your tire tracks to the parking area to complete the ride, **6.4** miles.

Gazetteer

Nearby camping: Denny Creek Campground, Crystal Springs Campground
Nearest food, drink, services: Snoqualmie Summit

28 Keechelus Lake

Distance	11.2 miles
Ride	Out & Back; wide gravel rail-trail; views
Duration	1 to 2 hours
Travel time	Seattle—1 hour; Ellensburg—1 hour
Hill factor	Flat; 60-foot gain
Skill level	Beginner
Season	Late spring, summer, fall
Maps	Green Trails: Snoqualmie Pass
Users	Bicyclists, hikers, equestrians
More info	Washington State Parks, 800-233-0321

The John Wayne Pioneer Trail cuts through rocks near Keechelus Lake

Prelude

The John Wayne Pioneer Trail, part of Iron Horse State Park, runs on an old railroad bed. The tracks and ties have been removed and the tread graded so that bicyclists, equestrians, and hikers can enjoy the wide rail-trail. The old railroad, the Chicago, Milwaukee, St. Paul, and Pacific, used to be part of the longest electric rail line in the country. Now this wide trail corridor provides recreationalists with easy access to the western shores of Keechelus Lake.

To Get There

From Seattle, drive east on Interstate 90 to exit 54, just past Snoqualmie Summit. Start your odometer at the end of the exit ramp. Turn right, then

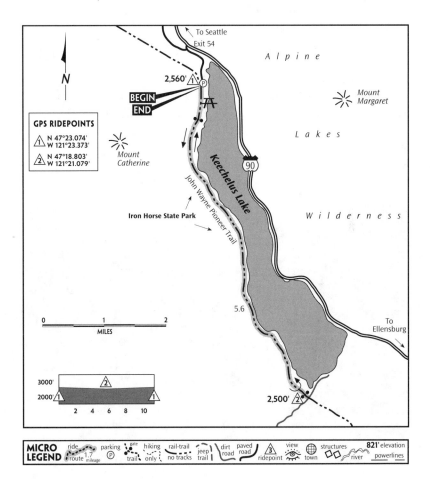

immediately left, following signs for Iron Horse State Park. At 0.5 mile, turn right, continuing toward Iron Horse State Park. Find Keechelus trailhead on the right at 1 mile.

The Ride

Begin by facing the rail-trail from the parking area; turn left onto John Wayne Pioneer Trail, pedaling east. At **0.4** mile, just before a white gate, pass by a picnic area below on the left, which overlooks Keechelus Lake. As you ride along the gravelly trail, you'll enjoy views of the lake. At **2.9** miles, the trail passes through a series of interesting cuts in the rock. Cross a short bridge at **4.2** miles. At **5** miles, the trail bends to the right, away from the lake. Pass over another bridge and then reach a white gate, **5.6** miles. From here, turn around and ride back to Keechelus trailhead to complete the ride, **11.2** miles.

Option

For cyclists raring to pedal some more, there are two options. First, you can continue east on the rail-trail, which, by the way, runs all the way to Idaho. Second, you can combine this ride with Ride 27, Snoqualmie Tunnel.

Gazetteer

Nearby camping: Denny Creek Campground, Crystal Springs Campground
Nearest food, drink, services: Snoqualmie Summit

SNOQUALMIE PASS
29 Mount Catherine
✿✿✿

Distance	16.2 miles
Ride	Loop; singletrack, jeep trail, dirt road; views
Duration	2 to 4 hours
Travel time	Seattle—1 hour; Ellensburg—1 hour
Hill factor	Several long dirt-road climbs; 1,080-foot gain
Skill level	Advanced
Season	Summer, fall
Maps	Green Trails: Snoqualmie Pass
Users	Bicyclists, hikers
More info	Wenatchee National Forest, Cle Elum District, 509-674-4411

Tiny lake at Windy Pass

Prelude

This area, chock-full of rugged jeep trails, raw singletrack, and dirt roads, has a lot of potential. Unfortunately, the U.S. Forest Service and the owners of Ski Acres have haphazardly developed the mountain-bike opportunities here. Despite the big races that are held each year at Snoqualmie Pass, poorly built and maintained trails, nonexistent signage, lousy maps, and too few

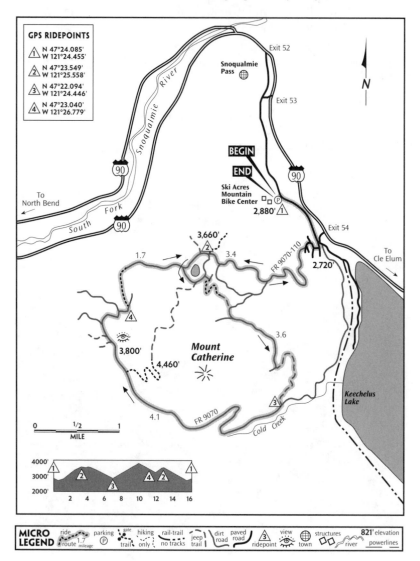

GPS RIDEPOINTS

⚠️1 N 47°24.085'
W 121°24.455'

⚠️2 N 47°23.549'
W 121°25.558'

⚠️3 N 47°22.094'
W 121°24.446'

⚠️4 N 47°23.040'
W 121°26.779'

MICRO LEGEND: ride route — 1.7 mileage | parking Ⓟ | gate — hiking trail | rail-trail no tracks ‑‑‑ | jeep trail | dirt road | paved road | 3 view ridepoint | structures ⊕ town | 821' river elevation powerlines

beginner and intermediate trails turn off a lot of potential cyclists. But there's big potential. This ride provides an overview of the possibilities: rocky, ragged, technical trails and doubletrack near Grand Junction and a series of dirt roads around Mount Catherine. Advanced riders should just go out and explore.

To Get There

From Seattle, drive east on Interstate 90, over Snoqualmie Pass, to exit 53. Start your odometer at the end of the interstate ramp, then turn right. Almost immediately reach a T and turn left. Pass Ski Acres on the right. At 1.4 miles, find the Ski Acres Mountain Bike Center parking lot on the right.

The Ride

From the parking area, ride back out to the paved road and turn right. Spin down the road to Hyak Ski Area, **0.7** mile, and turn right. Immediately, turn right again on Snoqualmie Drive. The climb begins here. Bear right at the fork, riding toward Forest Road 9070-110. Reach a fork in the road at **1** mile and bear left. Reach another fork at **1.2** miles and bear right. At **1.3** miles, turn right on FR 9070-110. When the dirt road forks at **1.5** miles, go right and continue the ascent. Ignore several lesser spur roads as you climb; stay on the main road. At **2.4** miles, pass straight through a four-way intersection on the main road. Ignore two lesser roads on the left as you climb.

At **3.4** miles, reach a five-way intersection named Grand Junction. From here, take a soft left onto (unmarked) Trail 7, a gravelly old road. At **3.5** miles, bear left at the fork. Descend to another fork at **3.7** miles, turn left, and ride up a steep, rocky road. Reach a T at **3.9** miles and turn left, descending on a rock and dirt road around the western side of aptly named Rockdale Lake. At **4.2** miles, take a hard right-hand turn onto a lesser dirt road. At **4.3** miles, reach a T and turn right. The doubletrack becomes a singletrack and then forks: Turn left. After a few more root-choked, muddy, technical turns, reach an intersection at **4.6** miles. Bear left onto the singletrack and descend to a wide gravel turnaround at the end of a road, **4.8** miles. Ride out the road to a T at **5** miles and turn right.

From the T, ride to a fork at **5.3** miles: Turn left. The road descends for a way, then climbs to a fork at **5.9** miles. Bear left on the lesser jeep track. The loose, rocky trail descends at a steep rate, and good riding skills are mandatory. The jeep track soon becomes a dirt road, and the riding gets easier. Reach a T at **7** miles. Turn right and begin riding up FR 9070. Pedal up the road, which ascends at a healthy grade. Ignore lesser spur roads as you climb.

At **9.7** miles, pass the trail to Mount Catherine on the right. Just up the road, pass an unmarked trail also on the right. Crest the top of Windy Pass at **10** miles. Just after the summit, ignore a lesser spur road on the left. At **10.4** miles, pedal by a tiny lake.

As the road descends from the lake, ignore several lesser roads on either side. But at a fork, **10.7** miles, go right. At **11** miles, reach another fork and bear right, crossing Olallie Creek. A few pedal strokes farther, take the left fork, which cuts a rocky descent. The rough road becomes a singletrack and weaves through a stand of trees. At **11.5** miles, the trail widens to a jeep trail again. The old road descends, passing trails on either side, then climbs. At **12.4** miles, pass a road on the right. At **12.6** miles, pass a road on the left. Return to Grand Junction at **12.8** miles. From here, take the same route back down to the parking area that you rode up at the beginning of the ride. Back at Ski Acres Mountain Bike Center, the completed loop measures **16.2** miles.

Gazetteer

Nearby camping: Denny Creek Campground, Crystal Springs Campground
Nearest food, drink, services: Snoqualmie Summit

MOUNT RAINIER

30 Carbon River Road

⊛⊛

Distance	10.6 miles
Ride	Out & Back; gated gravel road; short singletrack
Duration	1 to 2 hours
Travel time	Seattle—1.5 hours
Hill Factor	Gentle rise; 540-foot gain
Skill level	Beginner
Season	Late spring, summer, fall
Maps	Green Trails: Mount Rainier West
Users	Bicyclists, hikers
More info	Mount Rainier National Park, 360-569-2211

Prelude

Several years ago, a heavy storm washed away part of the Carbon River Road, which leads to Ipsut Creek Campground and several park trails on the northwest corner of Mount Rainier. Due to the damage, the National Park Service closed the last five miles of the road. This is great news for bicyclists, because

Old-growth forest near the Carbon River

we can now ride this easy, gently graded road along the Carbon River without worrying about vehicle traffic. When you arrive at the campground, the halfway point, you can park your bike and take one of several spectacular hiker-only trails that begin at the campground. However, not everyone wants the road to remain closed: According to the park supervisor's office, visitors, park employees, and Washington's congressional delegation are all split on whether to reopen the road. A decision will likely take several years or more, but now's the time for environmental organizations like the local Sierra Club chapter and Washington Trails Association to do something good for bicyclists and the environment, and lobby to keep the road closed.

To Get There

From Enumclaw, take State Route 410 southwest to Buckley. Zero your odometer in Buckley and proceed south on SR 165. At 1.7 miles, take the left fork, continuing south on SR 165. Pass through Wilkeson, 4.7 miles, and Carbonado, 7.1 miles. At 10.8 miles, take the left fork, following signs for the Carbon River entrance to Mount Rainier National Park. Reach the end of the

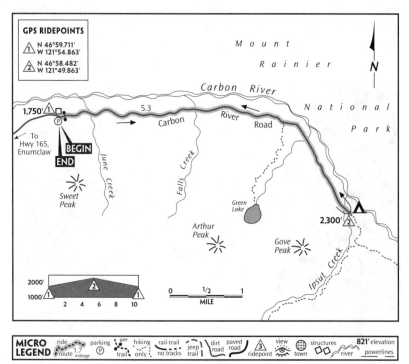

road at the old Carbon River ranger station, 18.9 miles.

The Ride

From the Carbon River ranger station, ride east on the wide, gated gravel road. The road rises at an almost imperceptible grade, through lush old growth and along Carbon River. At **1.7** miles, reach the section of road that has been washed out. Follow the narrow trail along the right edge of the gully before crossing the small stream twice. At **2.1** miles, the washed-out stretch ends and the trail pops up onto the gravel roadbed. Continue up the road. For a time, ride right along the edge of the milky, glacier-fed Carbon River. Soon, though, the

Ipsut Creek

road winds back into the mossy old growth. At **5** miles, the road crosses Ipsut Creek and enters Ipsut Creek Campground. Hiking trails begin at the end of the road, **5.3** miles. When you are done hiking, picnicking, or camping, turn around and ride back to the ranger station to complete the ride, **10.6** miles.

Gazetteer

Nearby camping: The Dalles Campground, Ipsut Creek Campground
Nearest food, drink, services: Carbonado

31 MOUNT RAINIER
Mud Mountain Rim Trail
⊕⊕⊕

Distance	7.6 miles
Ride	Out & Back; singletrack, dirt road
Duration	1 hour
Travel time	Seattle—1 hour; Yakima—2.5 hours
Hill factor	Several short climbs; 240-foot gain
Skill level	Intermediate
Season	Year-round (parking area closed September to March)
Maps	Green Trails: Enumclaw
Users	Bicyclists, hikers, equestrians on dirt road
More info	U.S. Army Corps of Engineers, 206-764-3750

Prelude

On any remotely nice summer day at Mud Mountain Dam Recreation Site—maintained by the U.S. Army Corps of Engineers—you'll see kids running across the grass, hurtling themselves toward swing sets, slides, jungle gyms,

Rim Trail with White River below

rope ladders, and a wading pool. The adult version of this—singletrack open to bicycles—begins nearby. If you're a parent, you'll have to flip with your spouse to see who gets to lie on the picnic blanket and watch the kids while the other (the winner?) hurtles toward the Rim Trail above the milk-colored White River. If you ride here with someone else, send them down the trail first. I rode this on a Friday, and it was pretty clear from the number of spiders that had set up camp across the trail that no one had ridden it for a few days. Here's a tip for solo riders: Ride with your mouth closed.

To Get There

From Enumclaw, drive east on State Route 410. After about 5 miles, turn right on Mud Mountain Dam Road, following the signs to the dam. Proceed 2.5 miles to the parking area at Mud Mountain Dam Recreation Site.

The Ride

From the parking area, ride back to the entrance gate and turn right on the wide trail that parallels the fence. After about fifty yards, the trail elbows to

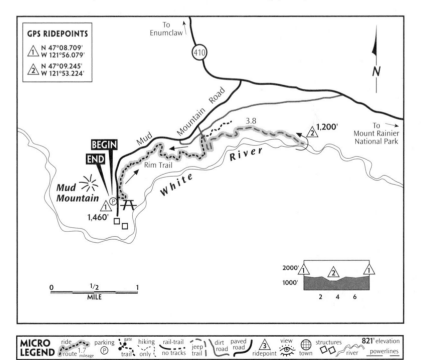

the left away from the fence and begins following the canyon rim. At **0.3** mile, the trail ends at a dirt road—turn right and ride down the road. At **0.5** mile, find the trail, which bends around a large cedar, on the left side of the road. Reach another road at **0.8** mile and turn right. Almost immediately you'll find the Rim Trail on the left.

From here, the trail descends for a short pitch, then noodles across a series of narrow wood planks that protect a boggy lowland. At **1.2** miles, the trail crosses a dirt road, bears to the left, and passes a small bathroom. After a few more turns, you will emerge from the dark forest and ride along a wooden fence that borders the cliffs that overlook the White River gorge. Pass a picnic table here, **1.4** miles. Just beyond the viewpoint, the trail bends away from the rim's edge and climbs for a short distance, possibly requiring a push. At **2.1** miles, reach a four-way intersection.

From this four-way intersection, several options present themselves. A left turn leads immediately into Weyerhaeuser's White River Tree Farm. Dirt roads and trails are everywhere. An interesting, though less maintained, trail crosses the road and continues along the river valley's rim. For the ride described here, however, turn right and glide down the dirt road, which switchbacks once on its way down to the banks of the White River, **2.9** miles. The dusty road continues upriver to the **3.8**-mile point, where it ends abruptly. Turn around here and ride back to the parking area, making the ride **7.6** miles.

Gazetteer

Nearby camping: Kanaskat-Palmer State Park, The Dalles Campground
Nearest food, drink, services: Enumclaw

32 Sun Top

⊗⊗⊗⊗

Distance	21.8 miles
Ride	Loop; singletrack, dirt road; views
Duration	4 to 7 hours
Travel time	Seattle—1.5 hours; Yakima—2 hours
Hill factor	Extreme 8-mile climb; 3,280-foot gain
Skill level	Advanced
Season	Summer, early fall
Maps	Green Trails: Greenwater
Users	Bicyclists, hikers, equestrians
More info	Mount Baker-Snoqualmie National Forest, White River District, 360-825-6585

Prelude

With seven skyscrapers' worth of elevation gain and a seriously technical singletrack, this ride comes pretty close to an epic rating. And if you aren't

A brief rest at the top of Trail 1183

physically and mentally prepared, you may well classify it as one. I took my brother on this ride (he had a new bike, but I guess it didn't come with new legs), and I don't think he's talked to me since. But the get-out views from the top, the sweet, high meadows, and the fast, corkscrewing descent make this ride a gem. Be careful not to blow out your legs on the long, torturous road climb that begins the ride, or you'll hate the best part.

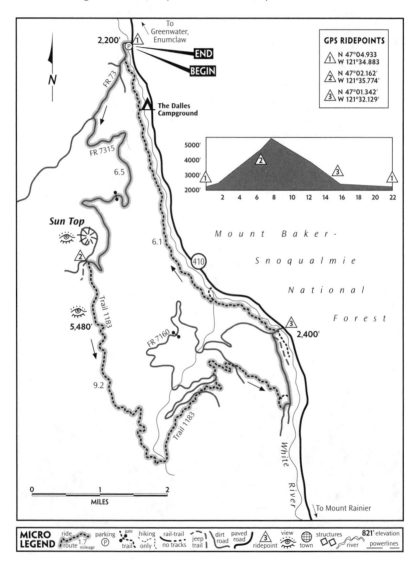

To Get There

From Enumclaw, take State Route 410 southeast toward Mount Rainier. After about 24 miles, find Forest Road 73 on the right. Park at this junction or at The Dalles Campground, which is located about 1 mile farther up SR 410.

The Ride

From the junction of SR 410 and FR 73, pedal up FR 73. Cross the White River and bear to the left, staying on the main road. When the road forks at **0.6** mile, bear right, again following the main road. At **1.4** miles, turn left on FR 7315 and begin the radical climb up toward Sun Top. Without a break, the road grinds and switchbacks up the north side of the mountain. Ignore lesser spur roads. At **3.5** miles, ride straight through the gate. At around the **4**-mile mark, using your natural tendency to make excuses, you'll convince yourself that your rear tire has gone flat. Just before a fork in the road, find Trail 1183 on the left at **6.5** miles. Turn left onto this trail. (If you want to bag Sun Top, turn right at the fork in the road, and pedal up the main road to the top, about one and a half miles away. While this spur adds 540 feet to the climb and slightly over three miles to the distance of this ride, the views from the lookout house are incredible.)

From the dirt road, Trail 1183 cuts due south, ascending an unnamed ridge that actually rises higher than Sun Top. This steep, narrow trail may prove a hike-a-bike. Several times it seems as though you've reached the top, but it's not until the **7.7**-mile mark that the sharp ridge is mastered. From the top, the trail traverses the precipitous eastern slope of the ridge. Open hillsides and rock escarpments give way to a thick forest as the trail undulates downward. At **10.2** miles, the trail forms an elbow bend as it crosses Buck Creek. After a fast, fun downhill traverse, cross a road at **11.4** miles.

Reach a fork in the trail at **11.7** miles, and bear left. At **12** miles, the trail widens to a jeep trail and veers left. Arrive at a dirt road (Buck Creek Road) and turn right, **12.1** miles. Just around the corner, **12.2** miles, Trail 1183 exits the road on the right. Take the trail. A few hundred yards further, enter a clearcut and reach a logging road that has obliterated the trail. Turn right, ride up the road a short distance, and find the trail continuing on the right. From here, the trail zigzags down a steep, rugged slope.

After a short traverse and several switchbacks, the trail crosses a road, **13.1** miles. Continue down the trail on the opposite side. Reach a fork at **13.6** miles—turn right. The way levels and winds through a thick wet forest. Arrive at a T, **14** miles, and turn right onto an old jeep trail, following the "trail" sign. In quick succession, turn right and then left. The jeep trail crosses a small creek and then ends at a dirt road, **14.2** miles—turn left. Stay on the main road as it bends to the left. Soon, the road runs along the edge of an airstrip. Just past the airstrip, **15.5** miles, reach Buck Creek Road and turn right. At **15.7** miles, just before crossing the White River, turn left onto Skookum Flats Trail 1194. (To save a lot of time, skip Skookum Flats Trail and ride down SR 410 to the junction with FR 73.)

Bagging Sun Top

At **16** miles, take the right fork, wrap around a tight turn, and cross a short bridge. From here the trail is quite technical, with awkwardly placed roots and tight turns, as it traverses a precipitous slope. Ride across a bridge at **16.8** miles. At **17** miles, a short, rocky, uphill section forces a push. At **17.1** miles, arrive at a fork: Go left, away from the river. (The right fork immediately uses a suspension bridge to cross the White River and leads to SR 410.) You'll likely have to walk much of the next one-quarter mile, up steps, roots, and large rocks. The trail levels out at **17.3** miles. At **17.5** miles, take the right fork and traverse the bank high above the river. The next several miles are technical and difficult, a hike-a-bike for less skilled cyclists. Ride through stands of old growth, with limited but lovely views of the White River.

After the **20**-mile point, the trail becomes less difficult. At **20.5** miles, reach a clearing and a campsite. From the camp, take the right fork on a wide trail, staying along the river. At **20.7** miles, the wide trail forks—again, go right, following the jeep trail. At **20.9** miles, the trail narrows to a singletrack again, weaving past some gigantic Douglas firs. **WHOA!** Stay on the main trail through this confusing section. At **21.5** miles, reach a gravel road. Turn right onto the road and quickly cross a paved bridge over the White River. At **21.8** miles, reach SR 410 to complete the loop.

Gazetteer

Nearby camping: The Dalles Campground, Silver Springs Campground
Nearest food, drink, services: Greenwater

33

Skookum Flats

✿✿✿✿

Distance	11.5 miles
Ride	Loop; singletrack, short dirt-road section
Duration	2 to 4 hours
Travel time	Seattle—1.5 hours; Yakima—2 hours
Hill factor	Short steep hills, some hike-a-bike; 200-foot gain
Skill level	Expert
Season	Summer
Maps	Green Trails: Greenwater
Users	Bicyclists, hikers
More info	Mount Baker-Snoqualmie National Forest, White River District, 360-825-6585

A smooth spot on the White River Trail

Prelude

This beautiful riverside trail winds through pockets of old growth along the steep western bank of White River. The trail is known to Northwest mountain bikers as one of the most relentlessly technical around, strewn with roots, rocks, and tight turns that all seem to be located at the edge of a sheer

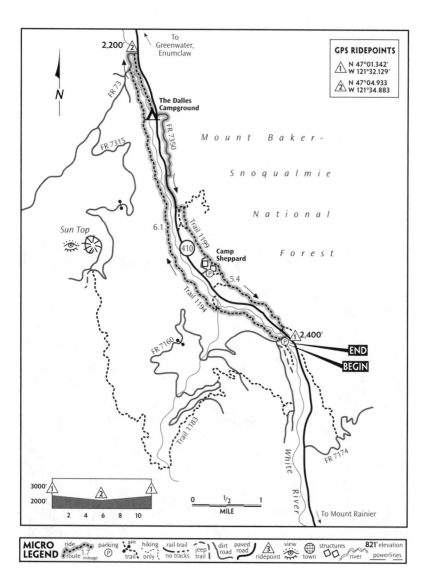

embankment. The dark forest and ravinelike quality of the river valley always makes me feel as though I'm riding this trail on a drizzly day.

To Get There

From Enumclaw, drive southeast on State Route 410. After just over 29 miles, turn right on Forest Road 7160 (Buck Creek Road). Immediately after crossing the White River, turn left into a small parking area.

The Ride

From the parking area, cross FR 7160 and find Skookum Flats Trail 1194, which exits the dirt road heading north. At **0.3** mile, take the right fork. After a tight turn, cross a little bridge. The trail traverses a steep slope high above the White River. Roots, rocks, tight turns, and a narrow tread demand advanced riding skills for the next five miles. Cross another wooden bridge at **1.1** miles. At **1.3** miles, reach a short, rocky ascent. At **1.4** miles, arrive at a fork: Turn left, away from the river. (The right fork immediately uses a suspension bridge to cross the White River and leads to SR 410.) You'll likely have to walk much of the next one-quarter mile, up steps, over roots, and around large rocks. The trail levels out at **1.6** miles. At **1.8** miles, take the right fork and traverse the bank high above the river. The next several miles are technical and difficult, a hike-a-bike for some. Ride through stands of huge trees, with limited but lovely views of the White River.

After the **4.5**-mile point, the trail becomes less difficult, and at **4.8** miles it enters a clearing at a campsite. From the camp, take the right fork, staying along the river. The trail is doubletrack at times, singletrack at others. At **5** miles, the road forks. Again, go right, following a wide trail. At **5.2** miles, the trail narrows again, winding past gigantic Douglas firs. WHOA! Stay on the main trail through this confusing section. At **5.8** miles, reach a gravel road, FR 73. Turn right onto the road and quickly cross a paved bridge over the White River. After the bridge, **5.9** miles, take Trail 1204A, which you'll find on the right. After some twists and turns and three short bridges, arrive at The Dalles Campground. At **6.4** miles, just before entering the campground, you'll find a 700-year-old Douglas fir that is nearly ten feet in diameter.

After a few "I am not worthys," ride across the narrow bridge and through the campground, staying to the left. Reach the entrance road to the campground at **6.9** miles. Turn left and immediately reach SR 410. Cross the highway and ride up FR 7150. At **7.1** miles, the road levels and bends to the right. Stay on the main road. At **8** miles, FR 7150 ends at SR 410. Turn left onto the highway. **WHOA!** At **8.6** miles, find a very faint, unmarked trail on the left side of the highway. This is an extremely difficult trail to find. Take the trail up a short bank away from SR 410, then parallel a small set of power lines. After a steep, but short, climb, the trail divides at the top, **8.8** miles. Turn left here, away from the power lines, onto White River Trail 1199. Ride through the woods, climbing to the **8.9**-mile point, where you'll find another trail junction. Stay on White River Trail. Reach another intersection at **9.2** miles: Again, continue straight on Trail 1199.

At **9.7** miles, enter a clearing at the edge of Camp Sheppard. The trail becomes a jeep trail here. But at **9.75** miles, where there are some buildings on the right, find a trail and a sign marked "trail" on the left. **WHOA!** This is a confusing section of the route. Take the trail on the left and then bear right, riding above the buildings at Camp Sheppard. After this turn, stay on the main trail. At **10** miles, arrive at another intersection: Continue straight on Trail 1199. At **10.3** miles, reach another intersection: Again, continue straight on Trail 1199. At **11.3** miles, arrive at yet another intersection: This time turn right, leaving White River Trail 1199. Ride about 40 yards down to SR 410. Cross it, turn left, and ride up the highway. At **11.4** miles, turn right onto FR 7160 (Buck Creek Road) and cross the White River. Find the small parking area on the left, **11.5** miles, to complete the ride.

Gazetteer

Nearby camping: Silver Springs Campground, The Dalles Campground
Nearest food, drink, services: Greenwater

34

MOUNT RAINIER
Ranger Creek
✦✦✦✦

Distance	18.4 miles
Ride	Loop; singletrack, dirt road; views
Duration	3 to 5 hours
Travel time	Seattle—1.5 hours; Yakima—2 hours
Hill factor	5-mile dirt-road grind, vertical descent; 3,020-foot gain
Skill level	Advanced
Season	Summer, fall
Maps	Green Trails: Greenwater, Lester
Users	Bicyclists, hikers, equestrians, vehicles on road
More info	Mount Baker–Snoqualmie National Forest, White River District, 360-825-6585

Dalles Ridge

Prelude

Even more radical than the climb up Sun Top (Ride 32), the dirt-road climb up to Corral Pass is just plain torture. But the smooth trail tread and beautiful scenery along Dalles Ridge help eclipse the pain of the ascent. Views into adjacent Norse Peak Wilderness and across the White River valley to Mount Rainier don't hurt either. I forgot to replace my brake pads before riding this

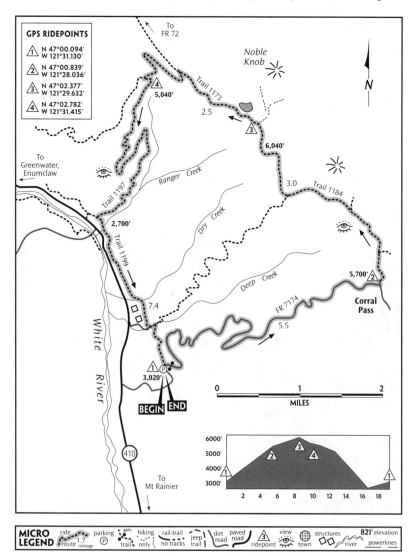

loop. Big mistake. My brakes screeched so loud during the nearly vertical descent off Dalles Ridge and down Ranger Creek that I was faced with the choice of going completely deaf or launching myself—due to excessive speed—into one of the large Douglas firs along the way.

To Get There

From Enumclaw, take State Route 410 southeast toward Mount Rainier. Just past milepost 56, turn left on Forest Road 7174 (Corral Pass Road). Start your odometer here and drive up this road about 0.7 mile. Park in a small dirt pullout (and trailhead) on the left just below a heavy gate.

The Ride

From the gate, ride up FR 7174. The unforgiving road zigzags up the steep western slope of Castle Mountain. It's on a grueling climb like this that cyclists rashly decide to spend hundreds of dollars on trick new equipment in order to shave a few ounces from the weight of their bikes. Many riders will need to stop several times to quell the hallucinations that the 3,020-foot gain precipitates. Stay on the obvious main road during the ascent, and watch out for vehicles. The road levels somewhat around the **5**-mile mark. At Corral Pass, **5.3** miles, reach a T and turn left.

When the road ends at the trailhead, **5.5** miles, take Noble Knob Trail 1184 on the right. The narrow trail traverses an open hillside. Reach a T at **6** miles, and turn left onto a doubletrack. The doubletrack narrows into a singletrack, levels, and continues to traverse north, riding the contours. This section of trail, atop a sparsely forested ridge, offers excellent views of Mount Rainier. Stay on the main trail, ignoring a few faint spurs. Reach a fork at **6.9** miles: Bear left on a narrow trail.

After a short walk to the top of a ridge that provides tremendous views of Norse Peak Wilderness and Mount Rainier, drop down a nice ridge trail to an intersection at **7.4** miles. Go right, staying on Noble Knob Trail 1184 toward 28 Mile Road. Ride through a beautiful, spare forest, traversing the high western side of Dalles Ridge. Beginning at **8.3** miles, the trail drops precipitously, and a short walk down several switchbacks is prudent to prevent erosion. Reach a T at **8.5** miles and turn left onto Dalles Ridge Trail 1173 (the Norse Peak Wilderness boundary is immediately to the right). A tiny lake sits in the swale below this intersection; on a clear day, the Olympics and Mount Baker are visible beyond several horizons of clearcuts.

The trail continues traversing this lower ridge, in and out of the trees, providing more wonderful views of Mount Rainier. At **9.7** miles the trail divides: take the left fork down Ranger Creek Trail 1197. The rough trail drops quickly, switchbacking for the next mile, and at **11** miles it reaches a wooden shelter. The trail forks here. From the shelter, take the left fork, continuing down Ranger Creek Trail 1197. Immediately the vertical drop begins. The trail is so steep and rough that the next couple miles may be a hike-a-bike for some riders. At **13.3** miles, bear to the left (a short trail spurs off to the right toward Little Ranger Peak Viewpoint).

From here the grade isn't quite as dramatic as the trail switchbacks through a dense forest, following the flow of Ranger Creek. Reach a T at **16.4** miles and turn left. At **16.5** miles, cross Ranger Creek. The trail climbs and descends on a tricky traverse above SR 410. At **17.8** miles, ignore a bridge across Deep Creek on the right and hike-a-bike up to a fork at **17.9** miles. Turn right here and cross this second bridge over the creek. After more climbing, a short traverse, and a section of technical riding, reach FR 7174, **18.4** miles, to complete the loop.

Gazetteer

Nearby camping: Silver Springs Campground, The Dalles Campground
Nearest food, drink, services: Greenwater

35
MOUNT RAINIER
Crystal Mountain
✿✿✿✿

Distance	14 miles
Ride	Loop; singletrack, doubletrack; views
Duration	3 to 6 hours
Travel time	Seattle—2 hours; Yakima—2 hours
Hill factor	Steep, rigorous climb, hike-a-bike; 2,620-foot gain
Skill level	Expert
Season	Summer, early fall
Maps	Green Trails: Bumping Lake, Mount Rainier East
Users	Bicyclists, hikers
More info	Mount Baker-Snoqualmie National Forest, White River District, 360-825-6585

Zipping Crystal Mountain singletrack (after cheeseburgers)

Prelude

I spent a hot July day riding this loop with a big group of friends. The steep, loose, at times rocky ascent proved too difficult for some in the group, so despite the beautiful day, they were having a bad time. But when we reached the summit house at the top of the ride, cheeseburgers were on the grill, ice-cold Pepsis were on tap, and a perfect view of Mount Rainier gave us all a powerful case of amnesia. After the rest break of fat and sugar, no one remembered the arduous climb. I suppose it didn't hurt that the singletrack from the top is one of my all-time favorites. Note: Rather than take the long trail to the top, some prefer the more direct though still difficult route on dirt roads (cat tracks in winter) from the base of the ski area. Others, perhaps we should call them the Weak-willed Ones, prefer to ride the chairlift to the

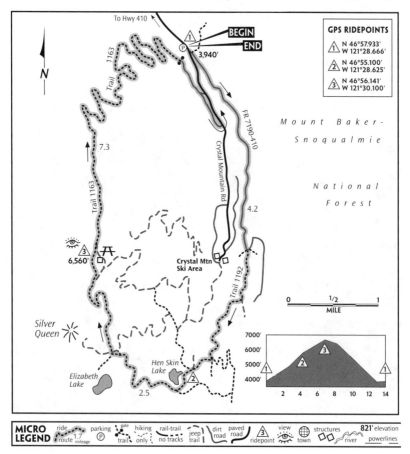

top. Definitely no cheeseburgers for them.

To Get There

From Enumclaw, take State Route 410 southeast toward Mount Rainier. About 33 miles from Enumclaw, turn left onto Crystal Mountain Road (don't enter Mount Rainier National Park). Start your odometer here. Drive up Crystal Mountain Road just over 4 miles and, as the road levels into the valley, park in a narrow pullout on the right side.

The Ride

From the pullout, continue riding up the paved Crystal Mountain Road. After just a few pedal strokes, turn left on FR 7190-410. Pass Norse Creek Trailhead and immediately begin the thigh-exploding climb. Traverse up the hillside, paralleling Crystal Mountain Road, below on the right. As the road begins a hairpin turn up to the left, three trails exit on the right, **2.3** miles. Take the middle one: Silver Creek Trail. The trail, narrow at times, wide at others, soon crosses an open ski slope.

At **2.6** miles, bear right, away from the jeep trail and onto a singletrack. A few spins farther, pedal into the woods and cross a bridge. Just across the bridge, you'll see the opening of a mine that disappears into the rock. From here, Silver Creek Trail 1192 traverses up at a stiff rate toward the head of the valley. Much of the next four miles will be a hike-a-bike for many riders. Reach a four-way intersection at **3.6** miles, and turn right toward Hen Skin Lake. At **4.1** miles, arrive at a fork above Crystal Mountain's Chair 4—turn left on the wide trail.

Reach Hen Skin Lake at **4.2** miles. Keep the lake on your right, ignoring numerous spur trails, and at the far end climb away from the lake. The trail, rough and technical, climbs past both Miners Lakes at **4.5** miles and **4.8** miles and continues up to a fork just before a jeep trail, **5.1** miles. Don't drop down to the jeep trail; instead, take the left fork toward Elizabeth Lake. At **5.2** miles, fork to the right, away from Elizabeth Lake. Pass under two chairlifts and by a couple of dirt roads.

The trail traverses up a steep gravelly slope, then switchbacks up to a saddle at **6.4** miles. Continue up and around, then at a dirt road take the trail on the left that cuts up a steep traverse behind the top of the mountain. Turn right on the dirt road near the top, **6.6** miles. At **6.7** miles, reach the top of the chairlift, with the summit house fifty yards to the right. (When it's open for business, you can buy cheeseburgers here and admire the panoramic view while you eat.)

To continue the ride, turn left, away from the summit house, and ride the ridge-top road toward a chairlift on the opposite side of the bowl. Continue east, riding behind the chairlift on a wide trail. A beautiful ridge-top traverse begins here. Stay on the main trail. Pass beyond the Crystal Mountain boundary, **7.6** miles. At a fork, **7.9** miles, go left. The trail soon begins wrapping from one side of the ridge to the other, across an open ridge with a few clusters of trees, before dropping down toward Crystal Mountain Road. **WHOA!** Watch out for equestrians on the descent. After a long series of switchbacks, reach a dirt parking area, **12.9** miles. Ride out the dirt road to Crystal Mountain Road and turn left. Ride down the paved road to the small pullout on the left, **14** miles, to complete the loop.

Option

Some cyclists prefer to ride this loop counterclockwise to avoid the long hike-a-bike stretch between the mine at 2.6 miles and the summit at 6.7 miles. However, the counterclockwise descent is rough, jarring, and much less enjoyable than the clockwise descent.

Gazetteer

Nearby camping: Silver Springs Campground, The Dalles Campground
Nearest food, drink, services: Greenwater

36
CLE ELUM
Lookout Mountain Epic
⊛⊛⊛⊛⊛

Distance	33.6 miles
Ride	Loop; singletrack; views
Duration	5 to 9 hours
Travel time	Ellensburg—40 minutes; Seattle—2 hours
Hill factor	Relentless up and down, much hike-a-bike; 3,060-foot gain
Skill level	Advanced
Season	Summer, fall
Maps	Green Trails: Cle Elum, Easton
Users	Bicyclists, motorcyclists, equestrians, hikers
More info	Wenatchee National Forest, Cle Elum District, 509-674-4411

Checking out the Yakima River valley from Cle Elum Ridge

Prelude

I readily admit that including this ride is cruel and unusual punishment. That said, I know there are plenty of Northwest riders who will hop on it as soon as the snow melts. Just be sure to do a few good training rides beforehand and then eat and drink constantly while you are out there. Now go hurt yourselves.

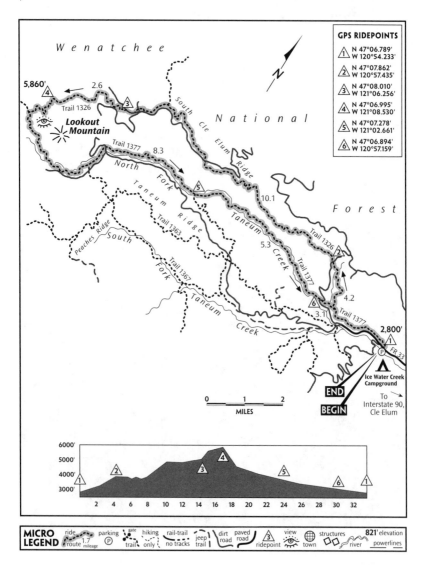

To Get There

From Seattle, take Interstate 90 eastbound past Cle Elum to exit 93. Start your odometer at the end of the exit ramp and turn left. At 0.3 mile, turn right on Thorp Prairie Road. At 3.9 miles, turn right on West Taneum Road and cross over I-90. At 4.1 miles, turn right, continuing on West Taneum Road. Stay on the main road, which becomes Forest Road 33, to Ice Water Creek Campground on the left at 13 miles. Park at the campground.

The Ride

Before setting out, be sure your pack is well loaded with sweet doughy things that contain lots of calories. From the junction of FR 33 and the entrance to Ice Water Creek Campground, take Trail 1377, which originates across FR 33 from the campground. Immediately the trail begins a short but steep climb (be prepared for 500 more of those). At **0.8** mile, the trail crosses a jeep trail. At **1.7** miles, reach an old beat-up road and bear right. When the old road forks, **1.8** miles, stay to the right, following the sign "North Fork Trail 1377/Cle Elum Ridge Trail 1326." As it ascends, the trail shifts between doubletrack and singletrack. Reach a fork at **2.5** miles and turn right on Cle Elum Ridge Trail 1326. From here, the trail grinds up the First Creek drainage. After crossing the creek and winding up a couple of switchbacks, reach a dirt road. Cross the road and continue up Trail 1326.

The trail continues its steep ascent up Cle Elum Ridge. Reach the top of a knoll at **4.9** miles and enjoy a short section of level riding. Stay on the main trail, ignoring several logging roads. At **5.5** miles, the sign reads "Windy Pass Trail 1326." For the next several miles, the trail, built by a local motorcycle club, twines frenetically up and down. Most riders will have to walk at least several sections of the trail. After more hike-a-biking, cross a dirt road at **7.9** miles. At **8.5** miles, reach a confluence of three logging roads; continue on the trail, following the signs toward Windy Pass. The hike-a-biking continues. Cross a dirt road at **9.2** miles.

The next five miles are difficult and require some patient route finding. Cross a dirt road at **9.5** miles. The trail affords nice views into the Yakima River valley. Drop a short distance and cross a dirt road at **10.5** miles. A few pedal strokes farther, cross another road. Follow the Cle Elum Ridge Trail signs; the trail parallels the road. After more views, ride down a series of switchbacks and cross a dirt road at **12.3** miles. Cross two more dirt roads, then at **13** miles, reach a fork in the trail—bear left toward Manastash Ridge. At **13.8** miles, the trail seems to end at a road: Turn right. After a few yards,

Fast smooth trail

turn left, back onto the trail. At **14** miles, the trail again seems to end at a dirt road. Turn right onto the road and begin riding up an extremely steep hill (my altimeter broke on this climb). At **14.3** miles, find a trail on the left and take it. Hike-a-bike up to a saddle at **14.5** miles, then ride across a timber harvest clearing next to a road. Though obliterated, the trail actually crosses the clearing (but not the road) and continues up the ridge.

Crest a high point at **14.9** miles and descend for a short distance. The trail heads up again, forcing more hike-a-biking, although less complicated route finding, as it edges around the north side of Lookout Mountain. Finally, the trail achieves the summit at **16.9** miles. The views from the top are tremendous. From here, the trail launches down a series of steep open-hillside switchbacks. Reach a fork at **17.4** miles and turn left on North Fork Trail 1377 toward Ice Water Creek Campground. For the next mile the trail corkscrews down a steep, technical set of unruly switchbacks.

Pass Taneum Shelter at **18.5** miles. From the shelter the descent is less severe, but the trail remains quite technical, with roots, mud, and numerous creek crossings. Ignore a trail on the right at **21** miles. Cross a dirt road at **22** miles. At **23.4** miles, ignore another trail on the right. Cross another dirt road at **24.1** miles. At **25.2** miles, pass Fishhook Flats Trail on the right: Continue down North Fork Trail 1377. From here the smooth trail roller-coasters along (and across) North Fork of Taneum Creek. This fast section is perhaps the most enjoyable stretch of the route. At **30.5** miles, the trail crosses a gravel road (if you've had it with singletrack, turn right and take the road back to Ice Water Creek Campground). Continue on the trail, descending toward First Creek. At **31.1** miles, reach a fork: Turn right. The trail widens and narrows and widens again as it drops. At **31.8** miles, stay left on the jeep trail. At **31.9** miles, take the trail on the left. At **32.8** miles, stay on the trail, which crosses a dirt road. The trail ends at FR 33 across from Ice Water Creek Campground to complete the loop, **33.6** miles.

Gazetteer

Nearby camping: Ice Water Creek Campground, lots of dispersed camping
Nearest food, drink, services: Cle Elum

37 North Fork Taneum Creek

☼☼☼

Distance	14.2 miles
Ride	Out & Back; singletrack
Duration	2 to 4 hours
Travel time	Ellensburg—40 minutes; Seattle—2 hours
Hill factor	Constant, fast-rolling trail; 740-foot gain
Skill level	Intermediate
Season	Spring, summer, fall
Maps	Green Trails: Cle Elum, Easton
Users	Bicyclists, motorcyclists, equestrians, hikers
More info	Wenatchee National Forest, Cle Elum District, 509-674-4411

Sunny day along North Fork Taneum Creek

Prelude

Fun and zippy, North Fork Taneum Creek Trail rises and falls along the creek. This is a great intermediate or advanced-beginner ride with lots of potential to add mileage and creek crossings if you feel like it. Just don't be put off by the first three miles, which are certainly the most difficult. You'll pass by no vistas, but the pine and fir forest and sprightly creek are lovely; the single-track, excellent.

To Get There

From Seattle, take Interstate 90 eastbound past Cle Elum to exit 93. Start your odometer at the end of the exit ramp and turn left. At 0.3 mile, turn right on Thorp Prairie Road. At 3.9 miles, turn right on West Taneum Road and cross

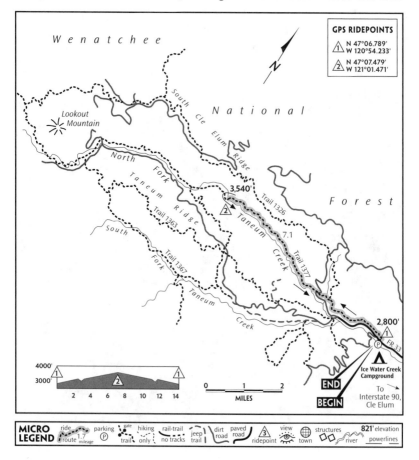

over I-90. At 4.1 miles, turn right, continuing on West Taneum Road. Stay on the main road, which becomes Forest Road 33, to Ice Water Creek Campground on the left at 13 miles. Park at the campground.

The Ride

From the junction of FR 33 and the entrance to Ice Water Creek Campground, take Trail 1377, which begins across FR 33 from the campground. The trail climbs a short but steep grade on a loose tread. At **0.8** mile, the trail crosses an old road. At **1.7** miles, reach a jeep trail and bear right. When the old road forks, **1.8** miles, stay to the right, following the signs toward North Fork Trail 1377. The trail, sometimes wide, sometimes narrow, climbs steadily. Reach a fork at **2.5** miles and turn left on North Fork Trail 1377. From here the trail is quite steep to the **3.1**-mile point, where it crosses a dirt road.

After the road crossing, Trail 1377 weaves through the woods, dropping and winding. Watch your speed because it's easy to get going too fast. The trail drops to the creek, climbs away from it, then zips back down again. Finally, after a lot of roller-coastering fun, the trail crosses the creek at **7.1** miles. Turn around here and retrace your pedal strokes back to Ice Water Creek Campground at **14.2** miles.

Option

To shorten this Out & Back and avoid the first three difficult miles, drive up FR 33, staying to the right at both forks, to the North Fork Taneum Creek Trailhead. To increase the distance, cross North Fork Taneum Creek at the 7.1-mile mark and continue out Trail 1377. The trail follows the creek about 8 more miles, getting progressively more technical, before it becomes really steep just past Taneum Shelter.

Gazetteer

Nearby camping: Ice Water Creek Campground, lots of dispersed camping
Nearest food, drink, services: Cle Elum

38

CLE ELUM
Fishhook Flats
⊕⊕⊕

Distance	19.1 miles
Ride	Loop; singletrack, dirt road
Duration	3 to 5 hours
Travel time	Ellensburg—40 minutes; Seattle—2 hours
Hill factor	Sharp climbs and descents, some walking; 1,440-foot gain
Skill level	Intermediate
Season	Spring, summer, fall
Maps	Green Trails: Cle Elum, Easton
Users	Bicyclists, motorcyclists, equestrians, hikers
More info	Wenatchee National Forest, Cle Elum District, 509-674-4411

Winding down the trail near Fishhook Flats

Prelude

For some not entirely clear reason, this is one of my favorite three-wheelers. The zippy singletrack, numerous stream crossings, and moderate elevation gain on this ride clearly outweigh the hardship of the hike-a-bike sections. Or maybe I just rode it in a good mood on a sunny day. For a weekend trip, combine Fishhook Flats with one of the longer, more difficult Taneum valley rides.

To Get There

From Seattle, take Interstate 90 eastbound past Cle Elum to exit 93. Zero your odometer at the end of the exit ramp and turn left. At 0.3 mile, turn right on Thorp Prairie Road. At 3.9 miles, turn right on West Taneum Road and cross over I-90. At 4.1 miles, turn right, continuing on West Taneum Road. Stay on the main road, which becomes Forest Road 33, to Ice Water Creek Campground on the left at 13 miles. Park at the campground.

The Ride

From the campground, continue up FR 33, which is paved. After **0.25** mile the road forks: Bear right on FR 33. When the road forks again at **1.7** miles, take the left spur, FR 3300, and immediately cross North Fork Taneum Creek. The dirt road heads up from the creek, quickly gaining big chunks of altitude. When the road forks at around the **2.2**-mile mark, turn left on lesser FR 135. At **2.7** miles, the road forks again: Stay to the right. From here the road drops toward South Fork Taneum Creek. **WHOA!** The road has crumbled away in places, making it impassable to cars and just dangerous for bicyclists. Ride along the creek for a short time at **3.3** miles, pass a dilapidated wood building, and begin climbing.

The road drops to the edge of the creek again and then climbs in earnest; between **4.4** miles and **5** miles, you'll burn a birthday cake full of calories. At **5** miles, reach a T and turn left on FR 3300. At **5.1** miles, abandon FR 3300 in favor of the lesser left fork, FR 3322, which heads toward South Fork Meadows. Descend quickly to a primitive camp area and a trailhead at the end of the road, **5.5** miles. South Fork Taneum Creek Trail 1367 begins here. The trail climbs above the north side of the meadow into thick forest.

The true singletrack climb begins soon after, when the trail forks at **5.8** miles. Turn right on Fishhook Flats Trail 1378 and begin the ascent. Some may hike-a-bike the next mile. Cross a dirt road at **6.4** miles. The vigorous grade continues until **6.8** miles, where it levels somewhat. Reach a four-way intersection at **7** miles: Ride straight through, continuing on Fishhook Flats

Trail 1378. The next few miles, through sparse forests and open meadows, are fast and enjoyable, with a little climbing thrown in for good measure. Enjoy it because you'll be pushing your bike up several switchbacks at the **9.1**-mile point. The walk proves short, and soon you'll be spinning again. Reach North Fork Taneum Creek at **10.5** miles. After crossing the creek, arrive at a T. Turn right on North Fork Trail 1377.

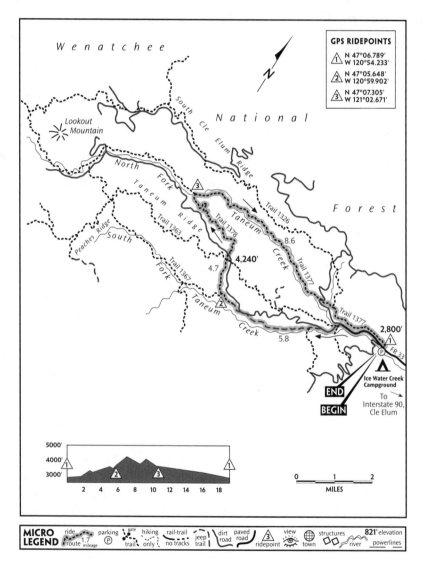

From here the smooth trail roller-coasters along (and across) North Fork of Taneum Creek. Over the next two miles you'll cross the creek six times, only once with the advantage of a bridge. At **16** miles, the trail crosses a gravel road. Continue on the trail, descending toward First Creek. At **16.6** miles, reach a fork: Turn right. The trail widens and narrows and widens again as it descends. At **17.3** miles, stay left on the jeep trail. At **17.4** miles, take the trail on the left. At **18.3** miles, stay on the trail, which crosses a dirt road. The trail ends at FR 33 across from Ice Water Creek Campground to complete the loop, **19.1** miles.

Gazetteer

Nearby camping: Ice Water Creek Campground, lots of dispersed camping
Nearest food, drink, services: Cle Elum

39 Taneum Ridge

◍◍◍◍

Distance	23.3 miles
Ride	Loop; singletrack, dirt road
Duration	4 to 6 hours
Travel time	Ellensburg—40 minutes; Seattle—2 hours
Hill factor	Much hike-a-bike, steep loose descent; 2,800-foot gain
Skill level	Advanced
Season	Late spring, summer, fall
Maps	Green Trails: Cle Elum, Easton
Users	Bicyclists, motorcyclists, equestrians, hikers
More info	Wenatchee National Forest, Cle Elum District, 509-674-4411

Closing in on the crest at Taneum Ridge

Prelude

This route, which passes along pristine creeks in beautiful forests as well as through barren clearcuts, is less traveled than either Ride 38, Fishhook Flats, or Ride 37, North Fork of Taneum Creek. Have fun out there, soak in the beauty, but ride with concern for the environment and an eye out for the safety of other trail users. Awkward route finding, a big elevation gain, lots of hike-a-biking, and rugged trails make this a challenging loop. Of course, it's better than any trail open to bicycles in neighboring North Bend Ranger District (since there aren't any), and the Cle Elum District should be commended for its commitment to shared trails.

To Get There

From Seattle, take Interstate 90 eastbound past Cle Elum to exit 93. Zero your odometer at the end of the exit ramp and turn left. At 0.3 mile, turn right on Thorp Prairie Road. At 3.9 miles, turn right on West Taneum Road and cross over I-90. At 4.1 miles, turn right, continuing on West Taneum Road. Stay on the main road, which becomes Forest Road 33, to Ice Water Creek Campground on the left at 13 miles. Park at the campground.

The Ride

From the entrance to the campground, ride out FR 33, which is paved. After **0.25** mile the road forks: Bear right on FR 33. When the road forks again at **1.7** miles, bear left on FR 3300, and immediately cross North Fork Taneum Creek. Just past the creek, pass a camping area on the left and Taneum Ridge Trail on the right. Ride up the dirt road, quickly gaining altitude. When the road forks at **2.2** miles, turn left on lesser FR 135. At **2.7** miles, the road forks again: Stay to the right. From here the road drops toward South Fork Taneum Creek. **WHOA!** The road has crumbled away in places, making it impassable to cars and just dangerous for bicyclists. Ride along the creek for a short time; at **3.3** miles, pass a dilapidated wood building, and begin climbing.

The road drops to the edge of the creek again and then climbs in earnest. At **5** miles, reach a T and turn left on FR 3300. At **5.1** miles, abandon FR 3300 in favor of the lesser fork on the left, FR 3322, which heads toward South Fork Meadows. Descend quickly to a tiny primitive camp area and a trailhead at the end of the road, **5.5** miles. South Fork Taneum Creek Trail 1367 begins here. The trail climbs above the north side of the meadow into thick forest. When the trail forks at **5.8** miles, stay on Trail 1367 to the left. The trail, muddy, rutted, and technical in spots, winds through a dark forest. At **7.2** miles, reach a creek crossing signed "Lame Horse Crossing" (so, does that refer to a lame horse or the lame crossing?). Try not to become lame yourself as you ford the creek.

After the next creek crossing, **7.5** miles, the trail forks: Stay on Trail 1367, taking the right fork toward Taneum Ridge Trail. I classify the next four miles as hike-a-bike, though much of it is ridable. Numerous creek crossings and a

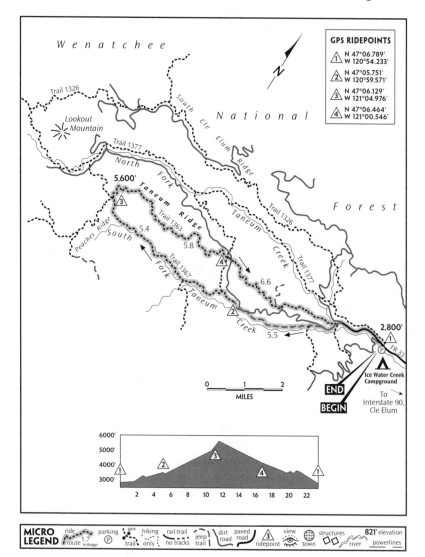

rough trail make the strenuous climb up South Fork Taneum Creek a technical challenge. At **9.7** miles, the trail bends to the right, away from the creek. The trail crosses dirt roads at **10.7** miles and then again at **10.8** miles. Reach a four-way intersection of trails at **10.9** miles: Turn right on Taneum Ridge Trail 1363. From the four-way, the trail cuts a series of steep switchbacks up the hillside. Thankfully, after a very tight righthand switchback, **11.4** miles, the trail levels somewhat. Victory is at hand.

Crest the top of the ridge at **11.6** miles. Cross a dirt road at **12** miles. At **16.7** miles, reach a four-way intersection (Fishhook Flats Trail 1378 runs perpendicularly here). Go straight, continuing on Trail 1363, which is wide at this point. Cross a dirt road at **16.8** miles. For the next several miles, the trail has been chopped up by road building and timber harvesting, so the route is difficult to follow. When the trail meets a jeep trail, **16.9** miles, bear right onto the jeep trail. At **17.1** miles, ignore an old road on the left—stay right. When the rough and bumpy jeep trail forks at **17.4** miles, bear to the right. At **17.5** miles, take the right fork again, this time onto a trail that switchbacks down an open, clearcut slope. At **17.6** miles, the trail crosses a dirt road and climbs.

After some ups and downs, the trail—loose, dusty, and rocky—descends at a fast rate. At **19.4** miles, the trail crosses a dirt road and also, for a time, parallels a dirt road. At **20.7** miles, cross a jeep trail: Ride straight through. Take the main trail, which forks left at **21** miles, then cuts a brake-screeching spiral down around a knoll. The trail ends at FR 3300, **21.5** miles. Turn left on FR 3300, cross North Fork Taneum Creek, then turn right on FR 33, which is paved. Pedal easily down the paved road to Ice Water Creek Campground to complete the loop, **23.3** miles.

Option

If desired, there are several great ways to add mileage onto this loop. At the 10.9-mile point, go straight on Trail 1367 and drop to North Fork Taneum Creek Trail 1377 and turn right. Or at the 16.7-mile mark, turn left on Fishhook Flats Trail 1378, ride to Trail 1377, and turn right. Or, for a true epic, turn left at the 10.9-mile point and ride out Peaches Ridge on Trail 1363 to Quartz Mountain. From there, use Green Trails maps to choose any of a number of ways to return to Ice Water Creek Campground.

Gazetteer

Nearby camping: Ice Water Creek Campground, lots of dispersed camping
Nearest food, drink, services: Cle Elum

40

S. Fork Manastash Creek

Distance	14.8 miles
Ride	Out & Back; singletrack, dirt road
Duration	2 to 4 hours
Travel time	Ellensburg—45 minutes; Seattle—3 hours
Hill factor	Long, moderate singletrack climb; 1,600-foot gain
Skill level	Intermediate
Season	Summer, fall
Maps	Green Trails: Cle Elum, Easton
Users	Bicyclists, motorcyclists, equestrians, hikers
More info	Wenatchee National Forest, Cle Elum District, 509-674-4411

South Fork Manastash Creek

Prelude

Manastash Creek valley, just one ridgeline south of the Taneum, has an abundance of terrific mountain-bike opportunities. This Out & Back route up South Fork of Manastash Creek toward Quartz Mountain is the only one described here, but plenty of singletrack trails and four-wheel-drive roads can be pieced together to create countless rides, both long and short. This seven-mile mostly singletrack climb along the creek to Quartz Mountain Campground traverses dry, open hillsides.

To Get There

From Seattle, drive east on Interstate 90 to Ellensburg and take exit 109. At the end of the ramp, turn right on Canyon Road. Turn left on Umtanum Road; start your odometer here. At 1.8 miles, turn right on Manastash Road. At 13.4 miles, as gravel replaces the paved surface, Manastash Road becomes Forest Road 31. Stay on the main road to a T at 24.3 miles. Turn left onto FR 3100 and proceed to Shoestring trailhead on the right, 26 miles.

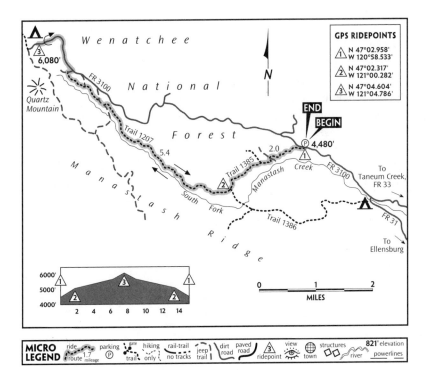

The Ride

From the trailhead, take Shoestring Trail 1385, which begins across FR 3100 from the parking area. The trail winds through the woods, then down along the lovely South Fork of Manastash Creek. At **0.9** mile, cross a dirt road. Reach an unmarked fork at **1.1** miles and bear left. At **1.3** miles, cross another dirt road and then climb. At **2** miles, the trail forks: Go right on Hereford Meadows Trail 1207. From here, the trail traverses to meet South Fork Manastash Creek again, then parallels the creek, climbing. Some sections of the trail are tricky and steep, but for the most part it's a smooth, ridable trail.

At **5.2** miles, the trail seems to end at a jeep trail. Turn right and ride up the jeep trail. At **5.3** miles, take the trail on the left. The trail seems to end at another jeep trail at **5.8** miles: Turn left onto the jeep trail, which soon becomes a singletrack. The trail ends for good at **6.2** miles. Turn right and ride up the dirt road. Reach a T at **6.4** miles and turn left onto FR 3100 (Quartz Mountain Road). Ride up this dirt road to the **7.4**-mile mark, where you'll find Quartz Mountain Campground on the right. From the primitive camp, turn around and pedal back the way you came to complete the Out & Back, **14.8** miles.

Option

From the campground, you can bag Quartz Mountain by climbing up FR 3100 to a trailhead, bearing left, and riding to the top, about one-half mile away. Quartz Mountain Campground also makes a great launching pad for epic rides north into either of the Taneum Creek drainages or southwest down to Little Naches River. Check out Green Trails' Easton map.

Gazetteer

Nearby camping: Buck Meadows Campground, lots of other primitive and dispersed sites
Nearest food, drink, services: Ellensburg

41 ELLENSBURG
Manastash Ridge
☼☼☼

Distance	14.3 miles
Ride	Loop; doubletrack, dirt road, paved road; views
Duration	1 to 2 hours
Travel time	Ellensburg—10 minutes; Seattle—2 hours
Hill factor	Steep 3-mile doubletrack climb; 1,780-foot gain
Skill level	Intermediate
Season	Spring, summer, fall
Maps	USGS: Ellensburg South, Manastash Creek
Users	Bicyclists, hikers, some motorized use
More info	Department of Fish and Wildlife, LT Murray State Wildlife Area, 509-575-2740

Doubletrack in the LT Murray State Wildlife Area

Prelude

Manastash Ridge is where Ellensburg locals go for their after-work mountain biking. Literally dozens of dirt roads and jeep tracks crisscross the wide ridge, part of the LT Murray State Wildlife Area. This ride offers up a sample of the area's potential, as well as its difficult route finding. Tall grass, sage, and chaparral vegetate the landscape until the very top of the route, where a scattered pine forest populates the ridge top. The lack of tree cover can mean a broiler, but it also provides great early season and late afternoon riding. And the open hillsides afford some unexpectedly fine views of the Yakima River valley, Ellensburg, and even the Alpine Lakes Wilderness.

To Get There

From Seattle, drive east on Interstate 90 to Ellensburg and take exit 109. At the end of the ramp, turn right on Canyon Road. Turn left on Umtanum Road; zero out your odometer here. At 1.8 miles, turn right on Manastash Road. At 3.3 miles, turn left on Strande Road, which is gravel. Turn left at the T. At

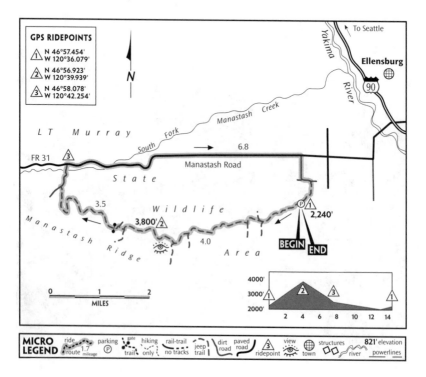

4.4 miles, take the right fork onto a rough dirt road. At around 5 miles, park alongside the road.

The Ride

Ride up the road, which becomes a doubletrack. When, after a one-mile warm-up, the doubletrack forks, bear right. Almost immediately, the doubletrack forks again—bear left. Reach a fork at **1.4** miles and bear right, continuing up. From here, the doubletrack gets steeper. But at **2.1** miles the grade levels somewhat. At **2.6** miles, crest the top of a knoll. But after a short, rocky descent, you'll be climbing again. At **2.9** miles, reach a fork and bear right on a well-worn jeep trail. At **3.3** miles, angle right at the fork and continue grinding up the ridgeline.

Reach the top at **4** miles—inspiring views all around. From the top, drop down a rocky doubletrack to a fork at **4.5** miles: Turn right. Climb a short distance into a sparse pine forest. At **4.6** miles, take the left fork, staying on the main road. Pass through a gate and then begin descending. After a fast series of turns, ride through a second gate on a rough, rutted trail, **5.4** miles. Reach a T at **7** miles and go right. After another fast descent, cross Manastash Creek and reach Manastash Road at **7.5** miles. Turn right on this paved road. At **13** miles, turn right on Strande Road. Turn left at the T, **13.5** miles. At **13.7** miles, turn right at the fork. Ride up the old dirt road to your car, parked alongside the road at **14.3** miles.

Gazetteer

Nearby camping: Buck Meadows Campground
Nearest food, drink, services: Ellensburg

42 Crab Creek

Distance	16 miles
Ride	Out & Back; wide gravel rail-trail
Duration	2 to 4 hours
Travel time	Yakima—1 hour; Seattle—2.5 hours
Hill factor	Nearly flat
Skill level	Beginner
Season	Fall, winter, spring (call for closure information)
Maps	USGS: Beverly SE, Smyrna
Users	Bicyclists, equestrians, hikers
More info	Washington State DNR, Southeast Region, 509-925-8510

Overlooking Lenice Lake

Prelude

Straight, flat, and sometimes sandy, this is somewhat of a mangy-dog ride. But like much in the desert, it takes time to appreciate the beauty here. You'll see few trees, but the Saddle Mountains rise impressively out of nothing to the south, and the series of lakes near the start will surprise most. Of course, a honed sense of adventure won't hurt either. In the end, I decided to include this ride because it's part of the epic cross-state trail, and we should be thankful to have it. For several years, this trail has been closed between June 15 and September 30; however, it may soon be open year-round (but beware of the summer heat). This section of the trail, managed by the Department of Natural Resources, requires a day-use permit, which is free. Call the DNR's Southeast Region offices to secure one.

To Get There

From Ellensburg, go east on Interstate 90 past Vantage. Take the first exit after crossing the Columbia River, and turn right onto State Route 26. Turn right again on SR 243, heading south for several miles. Immediately after

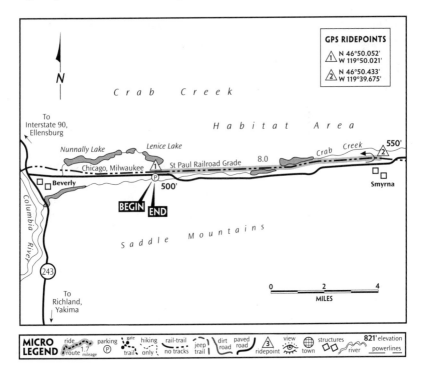

The rail-trail, an abandoned railroad line, paralleling the Saddle Mountains

passing under the old railroad trestle that spans the Columbia River, turn left. Start your odometer at this turn. Pass the hamlet of Beverly on the left. Drive 5.1 miles and find a trailhead and parking area on the left.

The Ride

From the parking area, a wide gravel trail leads to Lenice Lake (about one-quarter mile away), part of the Crab Creek State Wildlife Area. Instead, find the rail-trail, which runs perpendicularly to the Lenice Lake trail, and turn right. This ride, along the abandoned Chicago, Milwaukee, St. Paul Railroad line, is nothing if not straightforward. The route is flat and mostly straight. Parts of the trail may be quite sandy and brushy. Turn around at the tiny community of Smyrna, about **8** miles east of the Lenice Lake parking area. The return trip makes the ride **16** miles.

Gazetteer

Nearby camping: dispersed camping along Columbia River
Nearest food, drink, services: Beverly, Vantage

43 NACHES RIVER
Little Bald Mountain

⊕⊕⊕⊕

Distance	25.5 miles
Ride	Loop; singletrack, dirt road; views
Duration	3 to 5 hours
Travel time	Yakima—1 hour; Seattle—2.5 hours
Hill factor	Moderate grade up 11-mile climb; 2,870-foot gain
Skill level	Intermediate
Season	Summer, fall
Maps	Green Trails: Old Scab Mountain
Users	Bicyclists, motorcyclists, equestrians, hikers
More info	Wenatchee National Forest, Naches District, 509-653-2205

Prelude

I scouted this ride on a Saturday in August—during the flood of summer recreation—and I expected not only to choke on the dust kicked up by cars during the climb up to the trailhead, but also to see lots of mountain bikers out on the trail. Get this: I only passed two vehicles during the entire ten-mile dirt-road climb. Even more surprising—given that I like this singletrack descent better than either Sun Top (Ride 32) or Dungeness River (Ride 52)—I didn't see one other trail user. Not one. One sunny August Saturday plus one of the best, most picturesque singletrack descents equals zero other trail users. It doesn't compute. On the descent, views into William O. Douglas Wilderness and

Trail 961, routed along the edge of the cliffs

145

beyond into Mount Rainier National Park are extraordinary, as are the views of the Bumping River valley. For the high **WHOA!** factor on this ride, we can thank the trail builder who routed the trail along the edge of the cliffs.

To Get There

From Yakima, drive west on US Highway 12. About 5 miles past Naches, bear right and take State Route 410 for about 20 miles. Zero your odometer in

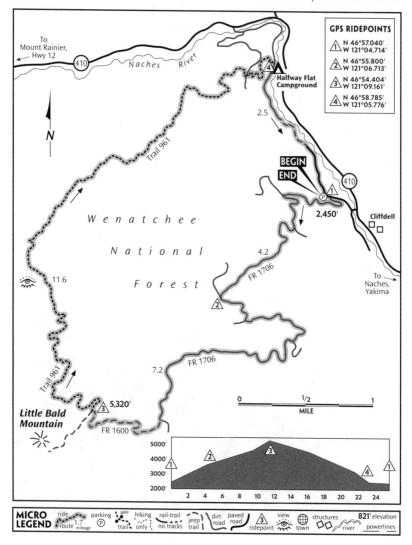

Cliffdell. At 0.7 mile, turn left onto Old River Road. Immediately cross the Naches River and turn right. At 1 mile, the road forks: Go right and park immediately on the left. (Alternate route: From Enumclaw, drive southwest on SR 410 over Chinook Pass. After about 23 miles from the pass, drive by Forest Road 19 on the left; start your odometer here. Continue southwest on SR 410. At 3.5 miles, turn right onto Old River Road. Immediately cross the Naches River and turn right. At 3.8 miles, the road forks: Go right and park immediately on the left.)

The Ride

From the parking area, ride back to the fork in the road and turn right onto gravel FR 1706, climbing up along Swamp Creek. The road climbs moderately. Stay on the main road as you climb. Reach a fork at **1.3** miles, and turn left, following the sign toward "Little Bald." At **2.2** miles, the road forks again; this time, go right. At **4.2** miles, reach a T—turn left to stay on FR 1706. Turn left at the next fork, **4.8** miles; then ignore the jeep trail that spurs off to the left at **5.8** miles. The road continues up at a moderate pace, through a successively thinner pine forest. As you climb, the sparse pine forest affords views through the trees. When the road forks again, **6.1** miles, continue on the main road, right.

At **9.6** miles, reach a fork and turn right onto FR 1600, following the sign: "Little Bald Mountain 3." From the fork, the road is less maintained and the grade angles up, switchbacking through a series of meadows spotted with pines. At a sweeping left-hand switchback just past the **11**-mile mark, watch for the trailhead on the right. Up ahead you'll see Little Bald Mountain and understand that it wasn't randomly named. (A side trip to the top of Little Bald Mountain is a nice touch; the views are spectacular, if you can stand the additional three-mile round trip and 700 feet of elevation gain.) Bald Mountain Trail 961 originates from a tiny pullout at **11.4** miles. The narrow trail charges down a steep slope to the north, switchbacking to a difficult rocky section at **11.7** miles. For less skilled riders, this scree slope traverse may require a short walk.

After the short stretch of scree, the trail cruises into the woods. From here, the trail is smooth and in good shape most of the way, with a consistent downhill grade that will keep a large grin on the face of the most curmudgeonly rider. You'll discover an excellent view of Mount Rainier and the William O. Douglas Wilderness at **13.6** miles—just a taste of what's to come. At **14.5** miles, the trail seems to end at a dirt road: Turn left and follow the

Mount Rainier beyond William O. Douglas Wilderness

primary dirt road. Find the trail on the left at **14.8** miles. Because of the clearcut of several years ago, the trails are not marked here, making this is a confusing section of the route. Once back on the trail, traverse across a clearcut bowl before entering the woods again. At **16.1** miles, a small sign on a tree to the left of the trail denotes the boundary of the William O. Douglas Wilderness. Off trail, just beyond the boundary on the left, cliffs drop off toward the Bumping River drainage. This is a great viewpoint.

WHOA! For the next four miles, the smooth singletrack flirts with the edge of the cliffs, offering both great views and radical exposure. This is one of the best extended stretches of singletrack anywhere. August heat waves rise from the top of the cliffs. This is the magical part of this ride. Finally, at **21.5** miles, the trail reaches a gravel road: Turn right, ride twenty yards to the turnaround, and take the faint, unmarked trail. (The trail is more technically demanding for the next mile and a half, so some riders may want to take the road, a less difficult alternate.) At **21.9** miles, the trail seems to reach a gravel road but actually bears to the right and continues down. The trail crosses a dirt road at **22.1** miles. At **23** miles, when Little Bald Mountain Trail ends at a dirt road, turn right and ride past Halfway Flat Campground and then along the Naches River.

At **24.1** miles, the road seems to end. Continue on the jeep trail beyond. The jeep trail ends for good 100 yards farther, where it's been washed out by the river. Though the situation appears dire, find a faint trail on the right and scramble along it to the other side of the washout. Pedal down the rocky road to a paved parking area at Boulder Cave Picnic Area, **24.6** miles. Ride down the paved road to the intersection with FR 1706 to complete the loop, **25.5** miles.

Gazetteer

Nearby camping: Halfway Flat Campground, Crow Creek Campground
Nearest food, drink, services: Cliffdell

44

NACHES RIVER
Crow Creek
✿✿✿✿

Distance	19.4 miles
Ride	Loop; singletrack
Duration	3 to 5 hours
Travel time	Yakima—1 hour; Seattle—2.5 hours
Hill factor	Constant, relentless up and down; 1,480-foot gain
Skill level	Advanced
Season	Summer, fall
Maps	Green Trails: Easton
Users	Bicyclists, motorcyclists, equestrians, hikers
More info	Wenatchee National Forest, Naches District, 509-653-2205

One of the few smooth, flat sections of Trail 941

Prelude

Pow! This adventurous, almost entirely singletrack ride packs a punch that you might not see coming from reading the ride statistics. The modest elevation gain and average ride distance falsely imply a less strenuous journey. Much of the sting arises from the first seven steeply roller-coasted miles on Pyramid Peak Trail. Rocks and loose dirt, a result of the heavy motorcycle use, make the trail difficult, not to mention dusty. The rest of the route features a more compact trail, but some of the climbs are hike-a-bikes. I rode this loop late on a hot, dusty summer afternoon and avoided much of the motorcycle traffic. However, I flatted on the epic descent (doh!) and, for many stupid reasons, ended up riding the last six miles on a flat. In twilight.

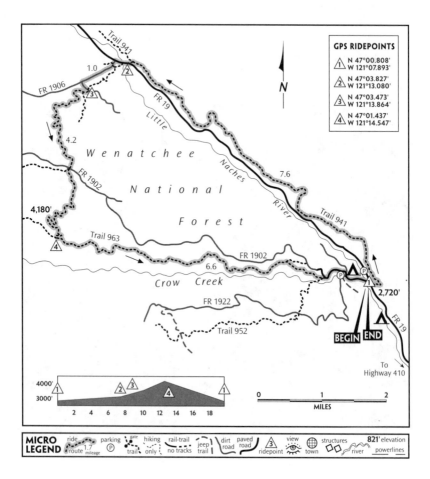

To Get There

From Yakima, drive west on US Highway 12. About 5 miles past Naches, bear right onto State Route 410. Drive to about 4 miles past Cliffdell and turn right on Forest Road 19 (Little Naches Road). Zero your odometer here. At 2.9 miles, find FR 1902 on the left. Park near this intersection. (Alternate route: From Enumclaw, drive southwest on SR 410 over Chinook Pass. About 23 miles from the pass, turn left on FR 19 (Little Naches Road) and start your odometer here. At 2.9 miles, find FR 1902 on the left. Park near this intersection, either along the road or by Crow Creek Campground, which is located a short distance up FR 1902.)

The Ride

From the junction of FR 19 and FR 1902, take Trail 941, which starts on the east side of the intersection opposite Little Naches River. The first one-quarter mile is quite steep, up a loose, rocky tread. Afterward, the trail drops and crosses a dirt road at **0.6** mile, then bridges Quartz Creek. The next seven miles are much like this first section to the bridge. At **0.7** mile, turn left at the fork. Cross another dirt road at **1** mile. Reach a fork at **1.1** miles and turn left, continuing on Pyramid Peak Trail 941. At **1.4** miles, take the right fork, continuing along the main trail. The trail crosses another road at **1.9** miles. Numerous trails cut by a few inconsiderate motorcyclists spur off and make the route finding difficult, so be careful to stay on the main trail.

At **2.6** miles, cross a dirt road. Be prepared for some walking due to steep grades and loose and rocky trail. At **3** miles, take the left fork. Just after crossing a bridge, go straight through a four-way intersection, **3.4** miles. At **3.8** miles, reach a dispersed campsite. WHOA! Bear right, pedal up a jeep trail, then immediately bear left on an unmarked trail. At **4.3** miles, ignore a trail that spurs down to FR 19. Go straight through a four-way intersection at **5.6** miles. When the trail forks at **6.2** miles, bear left and continue on Trail 941. At **6.3** miles, pass through a dirt parking area and then across a dirt road; silver diamonds and occasional trail signs mark the route.

At **7.5** miles, reach a fork and bear left, away from Trail 941. Reach paved FR 19 at **7.6** miles and turn right. (Note: You can ride singletrack rather than dirt roads for the next mile, but the maze of trails in this area makes the route finding quite difficult.) At **7.8** miles, turn left on FR 1906 (South Fork Road). Pedal along the gravel road to the **8.5**-mile mark and turn left on a dirt road. At **8.6** miles, turn right onto Trail 963. At **8.7** miles, reach a fork and bear right on Trail 963. After a short stretch of noodling through the woods, the well-maintained trail climbs at a vigorous (but ridable) rate, corkscrewing up cinder-block corners. Crest the wide, forested ridge at **10.3** miles, and begin a roller-coaster descent. Cross a dirt road at **10.5** miles and continue down the trail.

Reach a second dirt road, FR 1902, at **10.8** miles. Cross FR 1902 and ride through the dispersed camping area, following the signs for Trail 963A. Cross a bridge over Sand Creek and begin climbing. At **11** miles, cross a dirt road. From here the trail is relentlessly steep as it switchbacks south toward Crow Creek. It's a hike-a-bike to the high point at the **12.6**-mile mark. Traverse to a fork, **12.8** miles, and bear left on Trail 963.

Happiness follows as the descent paints a big smile on your face. The trail traverses down along the north rim of Crow Creek canyon. A few sections of the trail—steep, straight, and loose—require excellent bike-handling skills; try not to add to the already considerable trail damage. After the long descent levels somewhat, reach a fork at **17.4** miles and go right. At **17.8** miles, bear right at the fork. From here, stay to the right (but don't take Trail 952) until you reach FR 1902, then turn right and descend on this paved road. At **18.8** miles, reach a T: Turn right and cross the bridge over Crow Creek. At **18.9** miles, turn left and glide down FR 1902. Reach FR 19 at **19.4** miles to complete the loop.

Gazetteer

Nearby camping: Crow Creek Campground, lots of dispersed camping
Nearest food, drink, services: Cliffdell

NACHES RIVER

45 Raven Roost

⊕⊕⊕⊕

Distance	21.3 miles
Ride	Loop; singletrack, dirt road, paved road
Duration	3 to 5 hours
Travel time	Yakima—1 hour; Seattle—2.5 hours
Hill factor	Moderately difficult climb for 10 miles; 2,780-foot gain
Skill level	Advanced
Season	Summer, early fall
Maps	Green Trails: Easton, Lester
Users	Bicyclists, motorcyclists, equestrians, hikers
More info	Wenatchee National Forest, Naches District, 509-653-2205

Bridge across South Fork Little Naches River

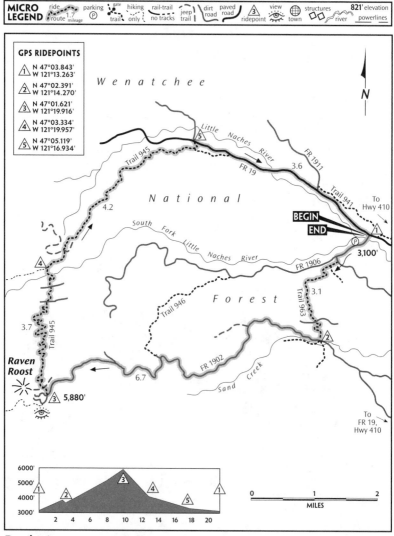

MICRO LEGEND: ride route — 1.7 mileage — parking P — gate — hiking trail only — rail-trail no tracks — jeep trail — dirt road — paved road — 3 ridepoint — view — town — structures — 821' elevation — river — powerlines

GPS RIDEPOINTS

△1 N 47°03.843'
   W 121°13.263'

△2 N 47°02.391'
   W 121°14.270'

△3 N 47°01.621'
   W 121°19.916'

△4 N 47°03.334'
   W 121°19.957'

△5 N 47°05.119'
   W 121°16.934'

Prelude

The long climb—up a singletrack and dirt-road route—to Raven Roost proves difficult but not frustratingly so. The grades are consistent, the tread well maintained. Even though it was a hot August day, I took only one break on the ascent because I didn't enjoy being given the five-times-over by the local flies. The ride offers a few views into adjacent valleys, but no grand views unless you take a short detour at the top for an awesome view into Norse

Looking east from Forest Road 1902

Peak Wilderness, with Mount Rainier as a backdrop. The technical, switch-backing, stair-stepping singletrack descent from the Roost—the Northwest's equivalent of Moab's Porcupine Rim Trail—will challenge even advanced riders, but, in the end, it administers a lot more fun than pain.

To Get There

From Yakima, drive west on US Highway 12. About 5 miles past Naches, bear right onto State Route 410. Drive about 4 miles past Cliffdell and turn right on Forest Road 19 (Little Naches Road). Start your odometer here. At 8.7 miles, find FR 1906 on the left. Park near this junction at one of the numerous pull-outs. (Alternate route: From Enumclaw, drive southwest on SR 410 over Chinook Pass. About 23 miles from the pass, turn left on FR 19 (Little Naches Road) and start your odometer. At 8.7 miles, find FR 1906 on the left. Park near this junction at one of the numerous pullouts.)

The Ride

From FR 19, begin pedaling out on FR 1906, South Fork of the Naches River Road. The incline is almost unnoticeable. At **0.7** mile, turn left onto a dirt road. Before the road can even make a turn, take Trail 963 on the right, **0.8** mile. At **0.9** mile, the trail forks: Take the right fork, continuing on Trail 963. This challenging singletrack climb requires several short pushes, but for the most part the steady grade and smooth tread will make you want to come back for more. The trail tops out at **2.6** miles, then descends to cross a dirt road, **2.7** miles.

The trail drops to FR 1902, **3.1** miles. Turn right and begin riding up the nicely graded road. Ignore lesser spur roads at **3.3** miles and **3.5** miles, and continue up the main road. At **6.8** miles, when the road forks, again follow the main road, left. (The right fork leads to the start of Trail 946, and this can be used to shorten the loop. See Option, below.) Continue climbing to a level traverse around the **7.4**-mile point. But beginning at **8** miles, the climb becomes steeper. Ignore lesser roads on the right at **8.1** miles and **8.4** miles. Finally, after a few territorial views and a nice mug of Raven Roost itself, the long ascent comes to a finish at a fork in the road, **9.8** miles. (Turn left and ride up a short distance to the viewpoint mentioned in the Prelude.)

At the fork, Trail 945 begins on the right. After a few innocently level twists and turns, the trail crosses a jeep trail and drops precipitously down a series of steep, yet quite ridable wooded switchbacks. From here, the skill quotient of the ride rises considerably, as the trail stair-steps down the slope, mimicking Moab's Porcupine Rim Trail. At **12.7** miles, where there's a clearcut on your left, cross a dirt road. Cross another road at **13.1** miles. From here the trail switchbacks steeply down to a bridge over South Fork of the Little Naches River. Across the bridge, the trail ascends rapidly, forcing a short hike to a T at **13.5** miles: Turn right.

The trail traverses now, following the slope across clearcuts toward Little Naches River. At **13.8** miles, cross an old dirt road with trailhead parking to the left. The trail crosses another road at **14** miles, skirting a clearcut. At **15.8** miles, the trail parallels a road for a time before crossing it twice. Cross yet another road at **16.7** miles. When the trail forks at **17.4** miles, take the left fork, continuing on Trail 945. Arrive at FR 19 at **17.7** miles. Turn right on the paved road and spin back to the junction of FR 19 and FR 1906 to complete the loop, **21.3** miles.

Option

For a 12.8-mile version with an 1,880-foot elevation gain (8.6 miles shorter and 900 feet less climbing), take Trail 946, which begins at the 6.8-mile point.

Gazetteer

Nearby camping: Crow Creek Campground, dispersed camping along FR 19
Nearest food, drink, services: Cliffdell

NACHES RIVER

46 West Fork Bear Creek
⊕⊕⊕

Distance	5.8 miles
Ride	Out & Back; singletrack
Duration	1 hour
Travel time	Yakima—1 hour; Seattle—2.5 hours
Hill factor	Rolling, a couple steep sections; 400-foot gain
Skill level	Intermediate
Season	Late spring, summer, fall
Maps	Green Trails: Easton, Lester
Users	Bicyclists, motorcyclists, equestrians, hikers
More info	Wenatchee National Forest, Naches District, 509-653-2205

Prelude

This proves that easy rides do in fact exist in the Little Naches River valley. In contrast to all the challenging trails in the area, West Fork of Bear Creek Trail offers a short, nonstrenuous Out & Back. Most of the route is level as the trail winds through the flats along the creek, but a few sections ascend steeply and will likely require short walks.

To Get There

From Yakima, drive west on US Highway 12. About 5 miles past Naches, bear right onto State Route 410. Drive about 4 miles past Cliffdell and turn right on Forest Road 19. Start your odometer here. At 9.9 miles, find FR 1911 on the right. Turn right on FR 1911 and park alongside the road. (Alternate route: From Enumclaw, drive southwest on SR 410 over Chinook Pass. About 23 miles from the pass, turn left on FR 19 (Little Naches Road) and start your odometer. At 9.9 miles, find FR 1911 (West Fork Bear Creek Road) on the right. Turn right on FR 1911 and park alongside the road.)

Focusing on a quick turn

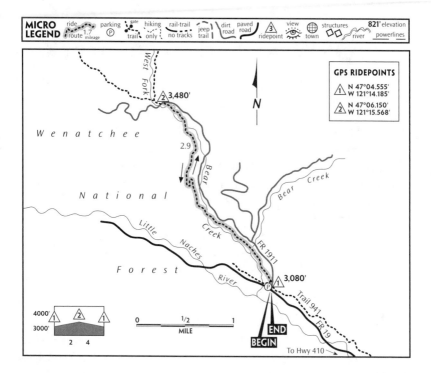

The Ride

Pedal up FR 1911. After a few hundred yards, find two trails on the left. Take the right-hand trail, Trail 943, which parallels the road. As you ride, ignore numerous trails on the right that access FR 1911. The trail crosses the creek several times. At **1.7** miles, you'll push your bike up a short hill. Descend back to the creek, and then cross it at **2.4** miles. When the trail kisses the road just after the creek crossing, bear left and stay on the trail. The trail crosses the creek several more times—a couple short pushes—and finally reaches FR 1911. The trail continues from here but gets quite steep. Instead, turn around and pedal back the way you came to make the ride **5.8** miles.

Gazetteer

Nearby camping: Crow Creek Campground, dispersed camping along FR 19
Nearest food, drink, services: Cliffdell

47
NACHES RIVER
Quartz Creek
⊕⊕⊕

Distance	10.1 miles
Ride	Loop; singletrack, dirt road
Duration	1 to 2 hours
Travel time	Yakima—1 hour; Seattle—2.5 hours
Hill Factor	A few difficult climbs and descents; 1,160-foot gain
Skill level	Intermediate
Season	Summer, fall
Maps	Green Trails: Easton
Users	Bicyclists, motorcyclists, equestrians, hikers
More info	Wenatchee National Forest, Naches District, 509-653-2205

The zippy, corkscrewing West Quartz Creek Trail

Prelude

The dirt road up to this ride's high point climbs the southern edge of Crow Creek canyon. Looking north across the canyon, you can imagine Trail 963 (see Ride 44, Crow Creek) dancing along the edge of the palisades. After achieving the crest and darting down a series of zippy singletrack twists and turns, West Fork Quartz Creek shows off some impressive palisades of its own. Be sure to stop before admiring the cliffs, because sections of the descent are extremely steep and technical, and you don't want to make any mistakes. The radical descents are quite short and can be easily walked by beginner and intermediate riders.

To Get There

From Yakima, drive west on US Highway 12. About 5 miles past Naches, bear right onto State Route 410. Drive about 4 miles past Cliffdell and turn right on Forest Road 19. Start your odometer here. At 2.9 miles, find FR 1902 on the left. Park near this intersection. (Alternate route: From Enumclaw, drive southwest on SR 410 over Chinook Pass. About 23 miles from the pass, turn

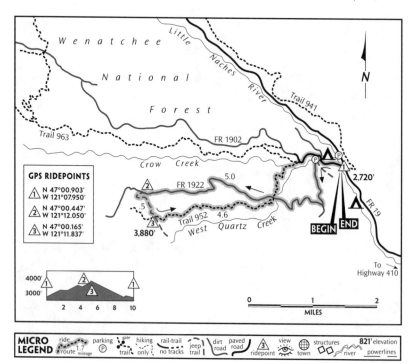

left on FR 19 (Little Naches Road) and start your odometer. At 2.9 miles, find FR 1902 on the left. Park near this intersection, either along the road or by Crow Creek Campground, which is located a short distance up FR 1902.)

The Ride

Start from the junction of FR 19 and FR 1902. Ride up FR 1902. At **0.4** mile, reach a fork in the road and turn left on FR 1920 toward Fifes Ridge. The road forks again just as the pavement ends—stay to the right and begin climbing. Stay on the main road as you ascend. When you reach a fork at **1.6** miles, go right on FR 1922. At **2.4** miles, the road passes by West Fork Quartz Creek Trail 952. Stay on the main road as you continue climbing. Soon, the road offers views to the right across Crow Creek canyon. At **5** miles, turn left on the lesser fork. This rough dirt road seems to go straight up; luckily, the road levels after about one-quarter mile.

At **5.5** miles, just before the road begins to descend, turn left on an unmarked trail. **WHOA!** This is an easy turn to miss. The smooth singletrack glides through the woods for a short way, then corkscrews down: a fun descent. At **8** miles, the trail crosses FR 1922. After the trail crosses the road, it becomes steeper and more technical. Some riders may have to walk down sections of the descent. Pass by the impressive Quartz Creek palisades. Cross several bridges around the **8.7**-mile mark. Cross Crow Creek at **9** miles and push your bike up to a T at **9.2** miles. Turn right and immediately reach a paved road, FR 1902. Turn right on the road and descend. Reach a T at **9.6** miles and turn right. Ride across Crow Creek and coast to a T, **9.7** miles. Turn left and ride back to FR 19 to complete the loop, **10.1** miles.

Gazetteer

Nearby camping: Crow Creek Campground, lots of dispersed camping
Nearest food, drink, services: Cliffdell

48

NACHES RIVER
Mount Clifty
✿✿✿✿

Distance	18.2 miles
Ride	Loop; singletrack, dirt road; views
Duration	3 to 6 hours
Travel time	Yakima—1 hour; Seattle—2.5 hours
Hill factor	Steep climbs and drops, lots of pushing; 2,500-foot gain
Skill level	Advanced
Season	Summer, fall
Maps	Green Trails: Easton
Users	Bicyclists, motorcyclists, equestrians, hikers
More info	Wenatchee National Forest, Naches District, 509-653-2205

The tortuous hike-a-bike route toward Mount Clifty

Prelude

I bonked on this ride, plain and simple. I'd like to say that I kicked it and was ready for a second ride that afternoon, but a deficit of calories squashed that idea like a little bug. I felt good on the five-mile dirt-road climb that begins the ride, but the Baby Ruth bar I ate at the start wore off. Not good. Manastash Ridge Trail takes off from the top of the road, and while it provides an

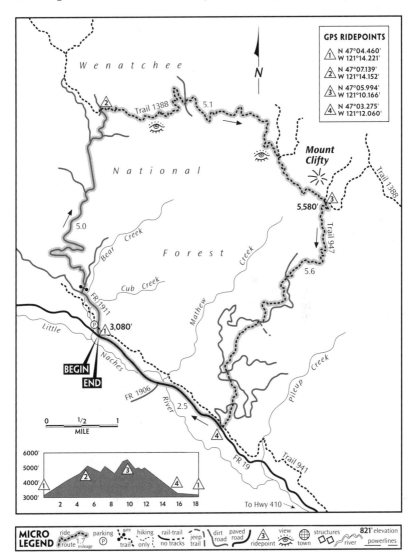

GPS RIDEPOINTS

⚠1 N 47°04.460'
W 121°14.221'

⚠2 N 47°07.139'
W 121°14.152'

⚠3 N 47°05.994'
W 121°10.166'

⚠4 N 47°03.275'
W 121°12.060'

MICRO LEGEND — ride route / 1.7 mileage — parking ℗ — gate / hiking trail only — rail-trail / no tracks — jeep trail — dirt road — paved road — ③ ridepoint — view 👁 town ⊕ — structures ⊡⊡ river — 821' elevation / powerlines

outstanding, continuous view of Mount Rainier to the southwest, the views weren't enough to propel me up and down this challenging, painful trail. Some sections of the trail are smooth singletrack, others rock-filled troughs caused by motorcycles. Many of the latter occur on uphill sections, requiring a fair amount of hike-a-bike. In fact, after some research I discovered this was the trail where an early mountain-bike pioneer coined the phrase "If you ain't hiking, you ain't mountain biking." From the top of the ride near Mount Clifty, trails exit in several directions. If you are interested in an epic ride option, check your Green Trails map. If not, you'll certainly enjoy the long descent back into the Little Naches River drainage.

To Get There

From Yakima, drive west on US Highway 12. About 5 miles past Naches, bear right onto State Route 410. Drive about 4 miles past Cliffdell and turn right on Forest Road 19 (Little Naches Road). Start your odometer here. At 9.9 miles, find FR 1911 on the right. Turn right on FR 1911 and park alongside the road. (Alternate route: From Enumclaw, drive southwest on SR 410 over Chinook Pass. About 23 miles from the pass, turn left on FR 19 (Little Naches Road) and start your odometer. At 9.9 miles, find FR 1911 on the right. Turn right on FR 1911 and park alongside the road.)

The Ride

Begin riding at the intersection of FR 19 and FR 1911. Ride up FR 1911, which is dirt, climbing gradually. When the road forks after crossing Bear Creek, **0.7** mile, turn right onto FR 1911-711. Pass through a gate to another fork in the road: This time, turn left. Let the climbing begin. Around a wide switchback at **2.4** miles, the pine forest thins, revealing a view of Mount Rainier. At **2.8** miles, the road levels somewhat before continuing up. Mount Clifty is visible on the right when the road enters a massive clearcut at **3.1** miles. The road forks at **3.4** miles and **4.2** miles; go right each time. The road, gravelly at times, forks again at **4.7** miles, and you need to take the left fork, which seems to go straight up.

Just as the road begins to level, **5** miles, you'll see a short road spur to the left. **WHOA!** Trail 1388—unmarked—crosses the intersection here. Turn right on the trail. After a short hike-a-bike, the trail, which varies from sandy to rocky to pine-needled, rolls and swells along the ridge top. After a particularly enjoyable descent, cross a dirt road, **7.9** miles. From here the trail climbs steadily, requiring a hike-a-bike on the rocky uphill traverse for over one mile. At **9.2** miles, with much of the worst climbing over, the trail forks—go right, following the sign toward Quartz Mountain. See Mount Clifty to the west, across the Greek Creek drainage. At **9.8** miles, the trail forks; go right. Less than one-quarter mile farther, ignore the trail that cuts back to the left.

At **10.1** miles, reach a four-way intersection. From here trails depart toward Windy Pass and the Taneum Creek drainage as well as Quartz Mountain and the Manastash Valley, for those interested in a truly epic ride. For this ride's route, however, stay to the right, following Trail 947 toward Naches. The trail drops sharply, and many of the switchbacks have been cut by lazy trail users. After the initial steep descent, the way winds downward at a more gradual rate, with some sections of short climbing mixed in. Cross a dirt road at **12.1** miles. At **13.2** miles, the trail reaches a dirt road just above a fork in the road—turn right and find the trail ahead, exiting the intersection between the forks. After a short climb, the trail spins down the ridge between Mathew and Pileup Creeks. Cross several dirt roads on the descent.

At **15.7** miles, reach the trailhead. For those with energy to spare, find Trail 941 to the right and ride it up to where it intersects with FR 1911. For everyone else, follow the short dirt road to FR 19, which is paved, and turn right. Either way reaches FR 1911 at **18.2** miles to complete the loop.

Gazetteer

Nearby camping: Crow Creek Campground, dispersed camping along FR 19
Nearest food, drink, services: Cliffdell

Riding the rolls and swells of the ridgetop west of Mount Clifty

49 YAKIMA
Cowiche Canyon
⚙⚙⚙

Distance	9.9 miles
Ride	Loop; singletrack, doubletrack
Duration	1 to 2 hours
Travel time	Yakima—10 minutes; Seattle—2.5 hours
Hill factor	Constantly rolling, one push; 450-foot gain
Skill level	Intermediate
Season	Spring, summer, fall
Maps	USGS: Wiley City, Yakima West
Users	Bicyclists, hikers, equestrians
More info	Department of Fish and Wildlife, 509-575-2740

Prelude

A squall blew in while I rode this high-desert loop, and I got soaked. Then I took a huge header on the way down to Cowiche Creek. Not happy. But the sun came out and I began darting around the tightly bunched maze of singletrack, doubletrack, and old jeep trails. The zippy turns and exciting trails brought my smile back. No epic views here, but the delicate desert flora juxtaposed with the ancient rock cliffs in the canyon make a lasting impression.

Typical Cowiche Canyon singletrack through a sage and rock landscape

To Get There

From Yakima, drive west on US Highway 12. Almost immediately, take the 40th Street exit and start your odometer. Travel 1.1 miles south on 40th Street. Turn right on Englewood. At 3.8 miles, turn right onto 80th Street. At 4 miles, turn left on Scenic, which is dirt. Park just before the stop sign at 4.5 miles.

The Ride

From the parking strip along Scenic, ride toward the stop sign. Just before the stop sign, find the trail between fences on the right. Do not ride up the private driveway on the right or you are liable to get shot. The trail climbs up a sagebrush-covered hillside. At **0.2** mile, follow the "trail" signs to the right. A few pedal strokes farther, cross a doubletrack and continue straight, following the "trail" signs. Reach a T at **0.3** mile and turn left. A few yards farther, turn right at the four-way intersection. At **0.4** mile, reach a jeep track that follows the ridgeline—bear to the right on the jeep track. Take the first left turn onto a doubletrack and begin climbing. Ignore a trail on the right; then, at **0.7** mile, reach a T at a fence: Turn right and continue climbing.

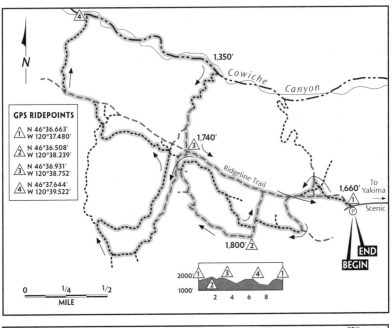

The doubletrack becomes a singletrack as it ascends. Pass a trail on the right. The singletrack ends at a doubletrack T, **1** mile. Turn left and keep climbing. When the way forks at **1.4** miles, bear right on the main trail. A few pedal strokes farther, the doubletrack forks again: Go right. The doubletrack descends and bears slightly right. Reach a T at **2** miles and turn right onto a narrow singletrack. The delicate trail weaves up the sagebrushy slope to a fork at **2.4** miles. Bear to the right and continue the ascent. Reach a T at a jeep track, **2.7** miles, and turn left. Ride down the jeep track to a T at the Ridgeline Trail, **3** miles. Turn left and ride west on along the ridgeline. Pass three trails on the left. Then at **3.5** miles, reach a four-way intersection and turn left onto a wide singletrack. Pass numerous trails as you descend; stay on the main trail.

After passing by several bike climbs on the right, reach a fork at **4.2** miles and bear right. At **4.3** miles, the trail forks at a fenced corner—bear right and follow the trail along the fenceline. Reach a T at **4.7** miles and turn right. You'll need to gear down and grind up this stretch of singletrack. When you arrive at a five-way intersection at **5.5** miles, take a hard left and noodle through a series of rocks. Reach a four-way intersection at **6** miles and ride straight through. At **6.3** miles, the singletrack ends at a T at the Ridgeline Trail: Turn left. Take the first trail on the right, **6.5** miles. This trail descends into Cowiche Canyon and finally reaches Cowiche Creek at **7.1** miles. An old railroad used to run along the river here, but the way has been converted into a rail-trail. Turn right onto the gravelly rail-trail and ride downriver. The rail-trail crosses and recrosses the river; high canyon walls frame the experience.

Cross the river four times. Just prior to the fifth bridge, find a narrow trail on the right, **8.1** miles. WHOA! It might be obscured by overgrowth. Take this trail and begin the steep climb out of the canyon. The first one-quarter mile is a push. The narrow trail widens considerably during the ascent. Ignore two trails on the right as you climb. At **8.7** miles, reach the Ridgeline Trail again and turn left. From here, ride the Ridgeline Trail straight back to the parking area to complete the loop, **9.9** miles.

Gazetteer

Nearby camping: Windy Point Campground
Nearest food, drink, services: Yakima

50 Cowiche Ridgeline
ΘΘ

Distance	4.4 miles
Ride	Out & Back; doubletrack
Duration	1 hour
Travel time	Yakima—10 minutes; Seattle—2.5 hours
Hill factor	A few gradual slopes; 80-foot gain
Skill level	Beginner
Season	Spring, summer, fall
Maps	USGS: Wiley City, Yakima West
Users	Bicyclists, hikers, equestrians
More info	Department of Fish and Wildlife, 509-575-2740

Prelude

This easy ridgeline jeep trail runs west and east on the wide ridge above Cowiche Canyon. There are many opportunities for adventurous beginning mountain bikers to try their hand at singletrack. In summer, be careful of excessively high temperatures and watch for snakes.

To Get There

From Yakima, drive west on US Highway 12. Almost immediately, take the 40th Street exit and start your odometer. Travel 1.1 miles south on 40th Street.

Squall brewing over Yakima

Turn right on Englewood. At 3.8 miles, turn right onto 80th Street. At 4 miles, turn left on Scenic, which is dirt. Park just before the stop sign at 4.5 miles.

The Ride

From the parking strip along Scenic, ride toward the stop sign. Just before the stop sign, find the trail between fences on the right. Do not ride up the private driveway on the right or you are liable to get shot. The trail climbs up a sagebrush-covered hillside. After about one-quarter mile, bear left on a jeep road. Stay on this main road, ignoring the numerous trails and doubletracks that spur off in either direction. The road, Ridgeline Trail, mounts the ridge that serves as the backbone of Cowiche Canyon Conservancy. The road ebbs and flows to a gate with a gravel pit beyond, **2.2** miles. Turn around here and ride the ridge back to the parking area to complete the Out & Back, **4.4** miles.

Gazetteer

Nearby camping: Windy Point Campground
Nearest food, drink, services: Yakima

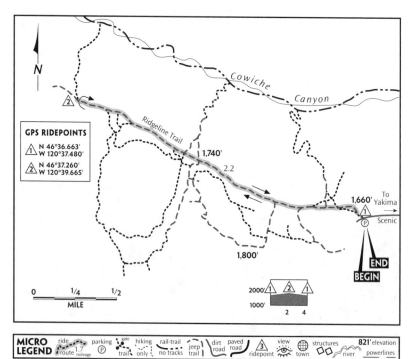

51

YAKIMA
Tieton River

⚙⚙

Distance	6.6 miles
Ride	Out & Back; singletrack, doubletrack
Duration	1 hour
Travel time	Yakima—30 minutes; Seattle—3 hours
Hill factor	Gentle up and down; 120-foot gain
Skill level	Intermediate
Season	Spring, summer, fall
Maps	Green Trails: Tieton
Users	Bicyclists, hikers
More info	Department of Fish and Wildlife, Oak Creek State Wildlife Area, 509-575-2740

Prelude

This is a nice, easy ride along Tieton River, through sagebrush and oak, in Oak Creek State Wildlife Area. Most of this ride travels on singletrack, but the tread is smooth and the grade gentle, thus the two-wheel rating.

To Get There

From Yakima, drive west on US Highway 12 to Naches. Start your odometer here, and proceed west. At 4.5 miles, turn left, continuing on US 12. At 6.6

Trail along Tieton River

miles, find Oak Creek State Wildlife Area on the right. Pull into the gravel lot and park.

The Ride

From the parking area at Oak Creek State Wildlife Area, carefully cross US 12. Cross the old, gated bridge that spans Tieton River. On the opposite bank, turn right and begin riding upriver. The doubletrack soon becomes a single-track, winding along the flats next to the river. To the left, cliffs shoot up from the valley floor. At **1.1** miles, bear left on the main trail. Pass by a steel bridge that crosses the Tieton, **1.8** miles. At **3.3** miles, reach a wooden bridge on the right that also crosses Tieton River. From here, the trail gets more challenging as it gains elevation. Turn around here and meander back to the Oak Creek parking area, **6.6** miles, to complete the trip.

Gazetteer

Nearby camping: Windy Point Campground
Nearest food, drink, services: Naches

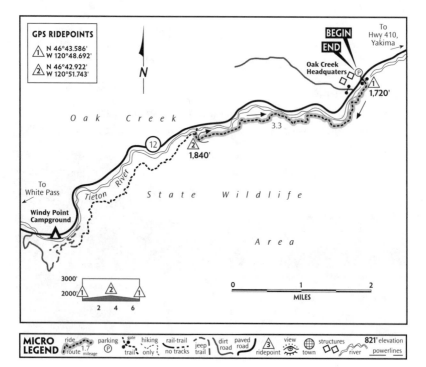

52 Dungeness River

⊕⊕⊕⊕

Distance	17.8 miles
Ride	Loop; singletrack
Duration	3 to 5 hours
Travel time	Seattle—2 hours
Hill factor	3-mile hike-a-bike, steep road climb; 2,000-foot gain
Skill level	Advanced
Season	Summer, fall
Maps	Green Trails: Tyler Peak
Users	Bicyclists, hikers
More info	Olympic National Forest, Quilcene District, 360-765-2200

Prelude

The rugged northeast corner of the Olympic National Forest is marked by dense forests and radical topography; Douglas fir and rhododendron cohabit the steep slopes above Dungeness River. The first three miles of this ride rate as a hike-a-bike. If you aren't feeling that ambitious, check out the Option section below.

Crossing the Dungeness River near the start of the ride

To Get There

Travel north on US Highway 101, past Quilcene and Discovery Bay. Just south of Sequim Bay State Park, turn left on Louella and start your odometer. At 0.9 mile, turn left on Palo Alto. When the road forks at 6.8 miles, bear left on Forest Road 28. At 7.7 miles, take the right fork on FR 2860. Pass East Crossing Campground on the right. Then at 10.8 miles, park alongside the road near Gold Creek trailhead.

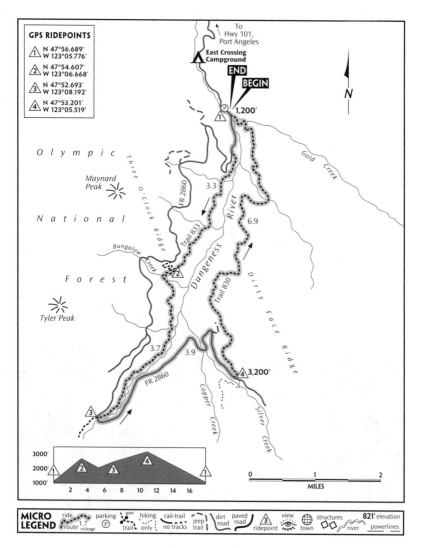

The Ride

From the parking spot alongside FR 2860, pedal up the road. At **0.5** mile, find Dungeness Trail on the left. After a few innocent rolls and swells, Dungeness Trail begins a hectic and stormy climb, traversing the precipitous slopes above the river. Plan on walking much of the next two miles; strong riders may call it a hike-a-bike. Pass a viewpoint at **2.3** miles. Reach a fork at **3.2** miles and bear left (see Option about the Three O'clock Ridge Trail, which is on the right).

From the fork, the trail tears down and around the lower edge of Three O'clock Ridge toward Bungalow Creek and, finally, to the bottom of the Dungeness River valley. Pass a wooden shelter on the left alongside the river at **5.2** miles. The somewhat technical trail ascends at the same rate as the river. Ignore a trail on the right at **6.8** miles. At **7** miles, reach FR 2860 and turn left. The road immediately crosses the river and begins a steep ascent. Stay on the main road as you climb. At **10.9** miles, just before reaching a dirt parking area on the right, find a trail on the left. Turn left here on Gold Creek Trail 830.

For the first several miles, the trail maintains a perfect downhill traverse—beautiful, fast, smooth, but not too steep. But when the trail reaches the precipitous side of Dirty Face Ridge, occasional pitches become quite steep. At **14.6** miles, reach a fork and bear left. After corkscrewing through a series of steep switchbacks, arrive at Gold Creek at **17.6** miles. You may have to ford the wide creek. The trail ends at FR 2860, **17.8** miles.

Option

To avoid the difficult three-mile hike-a-bike at the beginning of the ride: At the 0.5-mile mark, pass Dungeness Trail on the left and continue up the road. Stay on the main road, FR 2860, which climbs at a strenuous rate. After 4 miles, the road levels, then descends. At 5.1 miles, find Three O'clock Ridge Trail on the left. Take this narrow trail, switchbacking steeply down, to a T at 5.5 miles. Turn right. You are now at the 3.3-mile point of the basic, all-singletrack loop described above. This option adds 2.2 miles to the ride and 400 feet of additional climbing, but bypasses the hike-a-bike.

Gazetteer

Nearby camping: East Crossing Campground, Sequim Bay State Park
Nearest food, drink, services: Sequim

53

NORTH OLYMPIC PENINSULA
Spruce Railroad Trail

Distance	8.4 miles
Ride	Out & Back; singletrack; views
Duration	1 to 2 hours
Travel time	Seattle—3 hours; Bellingham—3.5 hours
Hill factor	Level with a few short easy hills; 100-foot gain
Skill level	Beginner
Season	Year-round (avoid during wet weather)
Maps	Green Trails: Lake Crescent
Users	Bicyclists, hikers
More info	Olympic National Park, 360-452-4501

Bridge along the Spruce Railroad Trail

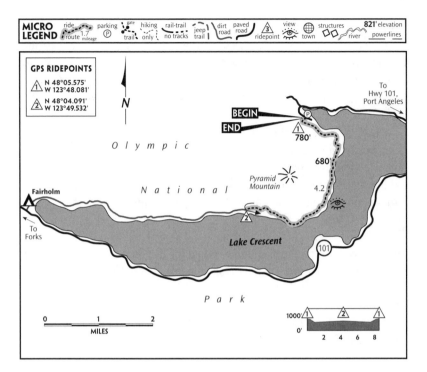

Prelude

I expected the Spruce Railroad Trail to be a lot like Iron Horse State Park's John Wayne Pioneer Trail—wide, gravelly, and nearly flat. Surprise! For most of the route, a singletrack follows the forested shore of Lake Crescent. Striking views of this beautiful lake can be found around every corner. The well-built trail and easy grades make this an excellent choice for singletrack first-timers or families.

To Get There

Drive east of Port Angeles on US Highway 101 for about 16 miles. Just past milepost 232, start your odometer and turn right onto East Beach Road toward Piedmont. At 3.4 miles, turn left, following the signs to Spruce Railroad Trail. At 4.3 miles, find the trail on the right and the small parking area on the left.

The Ride

Spruce Railroad Trail begins on wide, gravelly singletrack. But just past the **0.7**-mile mark, the trail narrows and descends to Lake Crescent—not a harrowing drop, but enough to make you feel a smile creep over that gritty bicycle face. Just past the **1**-mile point, the trail reaches the edge of the water, and startling lake views open up.

At **1.2** miles, cross a short bridge over a bonsai-sized inlet surrounded by rock cliffs. From here, a few technical sections will divert your eyes from the changing Lake Crescent views, but for the most part the singletrack is smooth and level. At **4.2** miles, reach a dirt road that denotes the western trailhead. Turn around and follow the trail back to the parking area, **8.4** miles.

Option

From the western trailhead, continue riding the dirt road to North Shore, 4.7 miles farther. Turn around here to make the ride 17.8 miles.

Gazetteer

Nearby camping: Elwha Campground, Heart of the Hills Campground
Nearest food, drink, services: Port Angeles

Not very easy. Trail disappears in places. Requires a lot of walking.

54

NORTH OLYMPIC PENINSULA

Lower Big Quilcene

✺✺✺

Distance	12.4 miles
Ride	Out & Back; singletrack
Duration	2 to 3 hours
Travel time	Seattle—2 hours; Bellingham—2.5 hours
Hill factor	Healthy singletrack climb; 1,040-foot gain
Skill level	Intermediate
Season	Summer, fall
Maps	Custom Correct: Buckhorn Wilderness
Users	Bicyclists, equestrians, hikers
More info	Olympic National Forest, Quilcene District, 360-765-2200

Descending the Lower Big Quilcene Trail

Prelude

During the dry season, the lower section of Big Quilcene Trail is perhaps the best singletrack ride on the Olympic Peninsula. Though a couple of rough, steep sections of trail may require short pushes, much of the route follows a smooth, pine-needled singletrack. The trail parallels the small but wild Big Quilcene River through a typical Northwest rain forest of moss, fern, Douglas fir, and cedar. The Bark Shanty Camp at the 2.8-mile point provides bike-and-camp possibilities.

To Get There

From Quilcene, drive south on US Highway 101. At 1 mile, fork right onto Penny Creek Road. At 2.5 miles, take the left fork, following the signs for Big

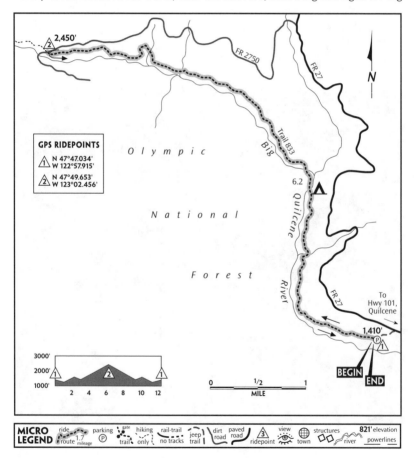

Quilcene Trail. This becomes Forest Road 27. Stay on FR 27, following the Big Quilcene Trail signs, until FR 2700-080 forks to the left at 6.1 miles. Turn left here. The road ends at the Lower Big Quilcene Trailhead, 6.5 miles.

The Ride

From the trailhead, perched above Big Quilcene River, take Lower Big Quilcene Trail 833. The trail, a nicely groomed singletrack, descends for the first mile. Because this is a popular route, watch for other trail users. The second mile rolls, with some easy climbs and dips. At **2** miles, cross a bridge over Big Quilcene River and begin a gentle climb. **WHOA!** The bridges are extremely slippery when wet. At **2.6** miles, pass Bark Shanty Camp on the right. Perched along the river, this beautiful campsite awaits those willing to pack in their gear. At **2.8** miles, cross Big Quilcene River a second time.

From here the trail gains elevation more steadily and becomes somewhat more technical as it follows the sharp river valley. At **5.1** miles, ride through (or ford, depending on the water flow) a small creek. At **6** miles, cross through another creek. At **6.2** miles, reach FR 2750. From here, turn around and ride back to the trailhead, **12.4** miles.

Gazetteer

Nearby camping: Falls View Campground, Rainbow Campground
Nearest food, drink, services: Quilcene

55 Beaver Pond Trail

ⵣⵣⵣ

Distance	9.3 miles
Ride	Loop; singletrack; views
Duration	1 to 3 hours
Travel time	Seattle—1.5 hours; Portland—3 hours
Hill factor	Some challenging singletrack climbs; 1,010-foot gain
Skill level	Intermediate
Season	Year-round
Maps	Washington State DNR: Green Mountain State Forest
Users	Bicyclists, equestrians, motorcyclists, hikers
More info	Washington State DNR, South Puget Sound Region, 360-825-1631

Enjoying Green Mountain State Forest

Prelude

The last time I rode the trails at Green Mountain State Forest, a group of three mountain bikers blew me off the trail. One of them came at me sideways, straightened out, and then bounced off a tree. It was the first time I'd ever had a bad experience with another trail user—no wonder hikers don't feel safe. I hope the evil bike genies break their bike frames before they hurt

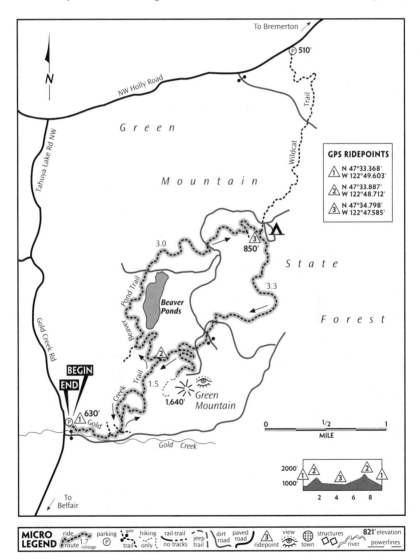

someone and give mountain biking a worse name. Though there are a number of challenging sections of trail along this short, three-wheel loop, most cyclists will enjoy it, especially the views from the top of Green Mountain on a clear day.

To Get There

From Tacoma, take State Route 16 north toward Bremerton. Just south of Bremerton, take SR 3 north beyond Bremerton to the Chico Way exit. At the end of the highway ramp, turn left onto Chico Way. Turn right onto Northlake Way, and then bear right onto Seabeck Highway and zero your odometer. At 3.2 miles, turn left onto Holly Road. At 7.6 miles, turn left on Tahuya Lake Drive. At 8.9 miles, bear left on Gold Creek Road. At 10.6 miles, pull in to Gold Creek trailhead on the left.

The Ride

From the trailhead, take the singletrack that parallels Gold Creek. At **0.4** mile, bear right. At **0.6** mile, turn left and begin climbing. Quickly reach a five-way intersection: Take a soft left-hand turn and continue the strenuous ascent. When you reach a fork at **0.9** mile, angle right. At **1.2** miles, reach another fork and bear right. Pass an old abandoned trail on the left at **1.4** miles and traverse. At **1.5** miles, take the sharp left on Beaver Pond Trail toward Green Mountain Camp. From here, the trail switchbacks down a lush hillside. Ignore an unmarked trail on the left at **2.1** miles. Pass by the beaver ponds, then cross a wooden bridge.

After noodling along a series of ponds, cross a dirt road at **2.7** miles. From here the trail is more challenging—winding, root-strewn, and narrow—and harder to follow. Ignore a faint trail on the left at **2.8** miles. When you reach a four-way intersection at **3.1** miles, continue straight on the trail. At **3.7** miles, cross a dirt road. At **4.2** miles, reach a T and turn left. When the trail forks a few pedal strokes farther, bear left. Reach a T, **4.5** miles, and turn right onto Wildcat Trail. From here, the sometimes rocky trail climbs steadily. On a clear day, you can see Puget Sound and Seattle off to the left at the **4.9**-mile point. At **5.1** miles, ignore a faint trail on the right. At **5.5** miles, the trail levels and descends along the high edge of a clearcut.

At **6.1** miles, reach a T at a dirt road: Turn right. After a few wheel rotations, find the trail again on the left. The singletrack ascends at a healthy rate to a four-way intersection of gravel roads at **6.3** miles. Bear slightly left to find the trail, which continues into the woods. At **6.5** miles, cross a road.

Reach a fork at **6.7** miles: Take a hard left onto Vista Trail and begin a technical, switchbacking climb. Arrive at a parking area at **7.1** miles. From here, the quarter-mile trail to the top of Green Mountain is closed to bicycles. Walk to the top to enjoy the excellent views of the Olympics on one side and Puget Sound on the other. Walk back down to the parking area, then resume your ride: switchback down Vista Trail to the previous fork, now **7.5** miles. Turn left at the fork.

At **7.8** miles, reach a fork and bear left (to the right is Beaver Pond Trail). At **7.9** miles, bear to the left again. At **8.1** miles, bear to the right and corkscrew down a steep, rough trail. Ignore the trail on the left at **8.3** miles. Return to the five-way intersection at **8.6** miles, and take a soft right. Pass by a trail on the left and then one on the right, then reach Gold Creek trailhead at **9.3** miles to complete the loop.

Gazetteer

Nearby camping: Scenic Beach State Park
Nearest food, drink, services: Bremerton

KITSAP PENINSULA

56 Twin Lakes Trail

⚙⚙⚙

Distance	15 miles
Ride	Loop; singletrack
Duration	2 to 4 hours
Travel time	Seattle—1.5 hours; Portland—3 hours
Hill factor	Rolling trail, a few short steep stretches; 280-foot gain
Skill level	Intermediate
Season	Year-round
Maps	Washington State DNR: Tahuya State Forest
Users	Bicyclists, motorcyclists, equestrians, hikers
More info	Washington State DNR, South Puget Sound Region, 360-825-1631

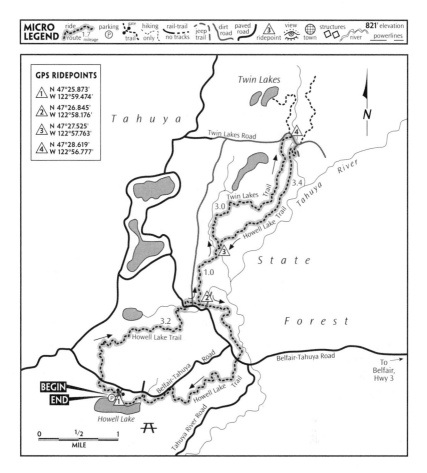

GPS RIDEPOINTS

⚠1 N 47°25.873'
W 122°59.474'

⚠2 N 47°26.845'
W 122°58.176'

⚠3 N 47°27.525'
W 122°57.763'

⚠4 N 47°28.619'
W 122°56.777'

Twin Lakes

Tahuya

Twin Lakes Road

Tahuya River

⚠4

3.4

Twin Lakes Trail

3.0

Howell Lake Trail

⚠3

State

1.0

⚠2

Forest

3.2

Howell Lake Trail

Belfair-Tahuya Road

To Belfair, Hwy 3

BEGIN
END

Ⓟ ⚠1

Belfair-Tahuya Road

Howell Lake Trail

Howell Lake

Tahuya River Road

0   1/2   1
MILE

N

Prelude

This loop, utilizing both the wide, gravelly Howell Lake Trail as well as the narrow, winding Twin Lakes Trail, provides a glimpse of what Tahuya State Forest has to offer. Almost 200 miles of official and unofficial trails crisscross the forest—plenty for the most fit cyclist and complete overkill for anyone with a poor sense of direction. Indeed, I've heard so many stories of cyclists getting lost out there, including several I tell about myself, that it's become the Tahuya joke. The trails range from easily negotiated dirt roads to expert-level singletrack (the last time I was out there, I broke a brake cable and was thankful for some of those wide, easy trails).

To Get There

From Tacoma, take State Route 16 north toward Bremerton. Turn left onto SR 3 and proceed south toward Belfair. At Belfair, turn right onto Northeast Clifton Lane; start your odometer here. Stay on the main road as Clifton becomes SR 300 and then North Shore Road. At 3.6 miles, turn right on Northeast Belfair-Tahuya Road. At 7.8 miles, turn left to stay on Belfair-Tahuya Road. At 9.5 miles, find Howell Lake Camp and Picnic Area on the left. (Alternate route: From Bremerton, drive west on SR 304, bear left onto SR 3, and travel south to Belfair.)

The Ride

From the picnic area, ride back up the entrance road toward Belfair-Tahuya Road. About 50 yards before Belfair-Tahuya Road, turn left onto Howell Lake Trail. At **0.25** mile, ignore a trail on the left. At **0.4** mile, pass a jeep trail on the right. Drop down a short hill and around a corner and cross Belfair-Tahuya Road. At the fork just after the crossing, take a right. From here, stay on the main trail. At **1.3** miles, take a left fork, following the diamonds and arrows. Again, stay on the main trail through second-growth fir and pine, with rhododendron, salal, and fern as ground cover. After following a creek for a short time, reach a fork—go left. After a bridge, cross a paved road at **3** miles, then quickly reach and cross a dirt road at **3.1** miles. When you reach a T at **3.2** miles, turn left.

From here the trail winds through a recent clearcut on a wide, banked-cornered singletrack. At **4** miles, the trail crosses a faint doubletrack, then heads into the woods. Cross a creek and head up a steep hill. At the fork just prior to the crest of the hill, turn left onto a narrow, unmarked singletrack. Almost immediately the trail forks again: Turn left on Twin Lakes Trail. This narrow trail weaves through salal and along an embankment. When the trail forks at **4.3** miles, bear left again. At **4.7** miles and again at **5.1** miles, take the right fork, both times staying on Twin Lakes Trail. At **5.3** miles, bear right on a wide gravel trail. At **5.6** miles, turn back to the left on the narrow dirt trail, Twin Lakes Trail. From here the trail is fairly challenging: a root-strewn, rocky climb.

Stay on the main trail, ignoring four lesser trails on the right. As you climb a hill at the **6.8**-mile point, the trail widens. Ignore several lesser trails on either side; stay on the wide, gravelly singletrack. At **7.1** miles, the trail elbows to the right. At **7.2** miles, reach a dirt road and turn right. The dirt road descends, crosses a creek, and then forks at **7.4** miles. Turn right onto the lesser doubletrack. **WHOA!** It's somewhat confusing through here—stay to the right. At **7.6** miles, take the trail back on the right. This drops to a bridge over the creek. Across the bridge, the trail—Howell Lake Trail—is wide and gravelly. Stay on this main trail to a fork at **8.4** miles. Bear left, continuing on Howell Lake Trail. At **8.7** miles, take the right fork. After a few more twists and turns, cross a bridge. Ignore three lesser trails on the right, then drop down and cross a creek. From here, ride the same trail back through the recent clearcut.

Reach a fork at **10.6** miles and bear left. Cross a dirt road at **10.8** miles, jogging to the left to regain the trail. After paralleling the Tahuya River for a short time, climb a hill and ride parallel to a paved road. The trail crosses the road—Belfair-Tahuya Road—at **12** miles. From here, the trail climbs much of the way back to Howell Lake; some sections may have to be walked. At **13.2** miles, ride straight through a four-way intersection. Cross several bridges along this stretch. After a particularly steep descent, turn left, away from the road. Just around the corner, **14.5** miles, reach a five-way intersection: Take the shallow left. At **14.9** miles, reach the entrance road to Howell Lake Camp and Picnic Area. Turn left and ride back to the picnic area to complete the loop, **15** miles.

Option

To add a couple more miles onto this loop, at the 7.2-mile point find the Twin Lakes Trail across the road to the left. Continue on that trail to Twin Lakes, about 1 mile farther.

Gazetteer

Nearby camping: Howell Lake Campground
Nearest food, drink, services: Belfair

57

Section 31

⚙⚙⚙

Distance	8.2 miles
Ride	Loop; singletrack, doubletrack, paved road
Duration	1 to 2 hours
Travel time	Seattle—1 hour; Portland—3 hours
Hill factor	Gentle topography, easy rolling hills; 120-foot gain
Skill level	Intermediate
Season	Year-round
Maps	USGS: Vashon
Users	Bicyclists, hikers, equestrians
More info	Washington State DNR, South Puget Sound Region, 360-825-1631

Trail through the scotch broom on Vashon Island

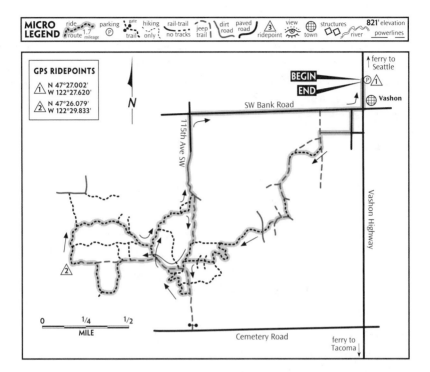

GPS RIDEPOINTS

1. N 47°27.002'
   W 122°27.620'

2. N 47°26.079'
   W 122°29.833'

N

115th Ave SW

ferry to Seattle

BEGIN

END

℗

Vashon

SW Bank Road

Vashon Highway

0   1/4   1/2
MILE

Cemetery Road

ferry to Tacoma

Prelude

While I was researching this ride, a Vashon Islander said to me, "Don't come over here, just leave your money on the boat." Fairly or unfairly, this quixotic statement both stereotypes and accurately describes many island residents. In a similar fashion, the confusing maze of trails on this DNR property, primarily located in Sections 31 and 36 on the Vashon Quadrangle, takes some time to understand. With so many forks, turns, and intersections, you may toss this book in the first bog you find and just ride, but this complicated loop provides a good introduction to the area and throwing this book in a bog would be bad. **WHOA!** In early summer the blackberry vines and nettles can be brutal, and many of the local riders use Slime (a puncture-resistant goo) in their inner tubes. In spring and fall, the trails here can be incredibly muddy. For insurance against face-planting into one of the deep mud bogs, you might consider riding with a snorkel. Free maps are available at the bike shop.

To Get There

From the Fauntleroy ferry dock in West Seattle, take the ferry to Vashon Island. Zero your odometer as soon as you exit the ferry. Follow Vashon Highway south for 4.9 miles. Two blocks shy of the four-way stop in the town of Vashon, find the bike shop on the left. Park here. (Note: This is a small parking area, so if you have more than two vehicles, find another place to park.)

The Ride

From the parking area at the bike shop, ride south on Vashon Highway. Reach a four-way stop at **0.2** mile and turn right on SW Bank Road. Take the next left on 100 Avenue Southwest, then take the following right on Southwest 178th Street. The road becomes gravel and then ends at a T, **0.4** mile. Turn left onto a gravelly doubletrack. Ignore a grassy doubletrack on the right at **0.5** mile; stay left on the main doubletrack. At **0.7** mile, find a raggedy singletrack into the brush on the right. After a few short turns, the trail runs alongside a ditch. At **0.8** mile, bear left, following the faint doubletrack. At **1.1** miles, ignore a doubletrack on the right—continue straight.

At **1.3** miles, bear to the right onto a singletrack (away from the "No Trespassing" signs). When the trail ends at a T, **1.5** miles, turn right onto the doubletrack. **WHOA!** Immediately take the left fork, then turn right onto a singletrack. Cross a dirt road at **1.6** miles and continue on the singletrack. Stay on the main trail. Walk around a very deep, perennial bog, **1.9** miles, and then immediately turn left onto a narrow singletrack. At **2.2** miles, reach a confusing section with numerous trails. Bear right on the main trail, riding west in the trough of the little valley. Pass several trails on either side that head up the hillsides. Reach a fork at **2.3** miles and bear left. At **2.4** miles, arrive at a four-way intersection and turn left on the wide gravel trail. Ignore trails on the left and then on the right at around the **2.5**-mile point.

At **2.6** miles, turn right on a narrow dirt trail (if you reach the blue gate, you've gone too far). The next one-half mile will put a smile on your face as the trail snakes through the woods. At **2.8** miles, reach a T and turn left. Reach another T at **2.9** miles and turn left again. At **3.1** miles, arrive at a T at the wide gravel trail: Turn left. At **3.2** miles, turn right onto a singletrack known as "Techmo." Bear right at the fork at **3.3** miles, then bear to the left at **3.5** miles. The trail splits at **3.6** miles, then reconnects at **3.7** miles. Just after the trail reconnects, reach a T at a dirt road—turn right, then immediately turn right again onto a doubletrack. The trail narrows, then forks at **4** miles. **WHOA!** Bear right at the next two forks that come in quick succession, before reaching a T at **4.2** miles. Turn left and immediately reach another T—this time turn right on a wide gravel trail.

Stay on the wide gravel trail, which descends. After a quick descent and a short climb, turn left on a singletrack at **4.6** miles. This winding dirt trail forks at **4.9** miles: Go right. Reach a T at **5** miles and turn left on the wide trail. The trail narrows to a singletrack at **5.1** miles. At **5.2** miles, reach a T near the out-of-sight city dump and turn right. Bear left at a fork at **5.3** miles. At **5.4** miles, reach a clearing and bear right, riding along the edge of the field. At **5.5** miles, turn right onto a narrow dirt trail. At **5.8** miles, bear right at the fork. Bear right again at **5.9** miles. Take the next two left turns. The second left puts you onto Techmo again. Ignore a trail on the right at **6.3** miles. Reach a T at a dirt road, 115th Avenue Southwest, at **6.5** miles and turn left. Stay on the main road. At **7** miles, reach Southwest Bank Road and turn right. Stay on this road to the four-way stop in Vashon, **8** miles. Turn left onto Vashon Highway and ride back to the parking area to complete the ride, **8.2** miles.

Option

If you park at the Fauntleroy ferry dock and begin the ride from there, you will (a) be certain of making it onto the next ferry, (b) get a better workout, (c) not have to pay a fare for your car, and (d) avoid paying the overheight rate if you have a roof rack. Use the driving directions to add nearly ten miles onto the ride.

Gazetteer

Nearby camping: Dash Point State Park, Manchester State Park
Nearest food, drink, services: Vashon

58 S. Fork Skokomish River

☺☺☺

Distance	17.8 miles
Ride	Out & Back; singletrack
Duration	3 to 5 hours
Travel time	Seattle—2 hours, Portland—3 hours
Hill factor	Gradual singletrack climb, some walking; 400-foot gain
Skill level	Intermediate
Season	Spring, summer, fall
Maps	Custom Correct: Mount Skokomish
Users	Bicyclists, equestrians, hikers
More info	Olympic National Forest, Hood Canal District, 360-877-5254

Gliding along Trail 873

Prelude

While not classified as a *views* ride, this Out & Back ride along South Fork of the Skokomish River is magically beautiful. The well-maintained trail winds along the powerful river, which flows around to the south of Mount Tebo. The first four miles are quite easy; afterward, plan on some walking to the turn-around point.

To Get There

From Olympia, drive north on US Highway 101 past Shelton. At the junction of US 101 and Skokomish Valley Road, start your odometer. Turn left on Skokomish Valley Road. At 5.8 miles, take the right fork on Forest Road 23 toward Brown Creek Campground. At 8.2 miles, take the left fork, continuing

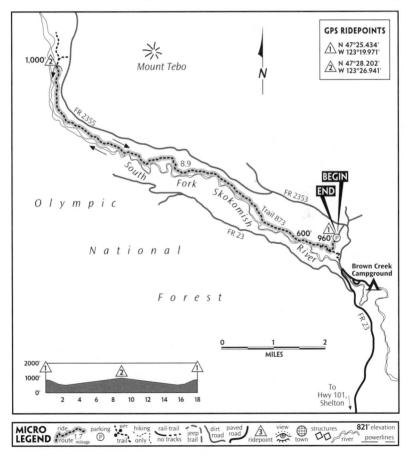

on FR 23. Stay on FR 23 to the 15.5-mile point, then turn right on FR 2354 toward Brown Creek Campground. Cross Skokomish River and turn left, 16.3 miles. Pass the lower trailhead on the left and continue up the hill. At 17.2 miles, turn left at the fork, then immediately take a second left turn. Proceed a short way to Skokomish Trail 873 trailhead.

The Ride

From the upper trailhead, ride out on Skokomish River Trail 873. At **0.2** mile, reach a T and turn right. The trail descends through big, mossy old growth into the flats along the river. Noodle through the lush lowlands of the Skokomish River floodplain, along the river and away from it. At **3.2** miles, cross a bridge by a gentle waterfall. After the **4**-mile mark, the trail becomes somewhat more technical, with some surprising climbs and, at times, a rough tread. Pass Laney Camp on the left at **8.2** miles. Reach the horse ford at **8.9** miles. From here the trail becomes more primitive. Turn around and enjoy the glide back to the upper trailhead, **17.8** miles.

Option

The bailout option: Just past the horse ford, you'll find a primitive trail on the right that cuts up the bank. Scramble up this steep trail to a dirt road and turn right. After a short distance, bear right on FR 2355 and ride back to the trailhead. This route is about one mile shorter and, because it's a road ride, much faster.

Gazetteer

Nearby camping: Brown Creek Campground
Nearest food, drink, services: Potlatch, Shelton

59 Wynoochee Lake

⊕⊕⊕⊕

Distance	12.9 miles
Ride	Loop; singletrack
Duration	3 to 5 hours
Travel time	Seattle—3 hours; Portland—3.5 hours
Hill factor	Moderate up and down, some hike-a-bike; 160-foot gain
Skill level	Intermediate
Season	Summer, fall
Maps	USGS: Wynoochee Lake
Users	Bicyclists, hikers
More info	Olympic National Forest, Hood Canal District, 360-877-5254

Wynooching across the river at Ridepoint 2

Prelude

The loop around Wynoochee Lake is great fun if you're in an adventurous mood. Much of the way travels over smooth, zippy singletrack, but numerous washouts require some scrambling, and then there's that river you have to ford. Promised trail maintenance and a new bridge will add about four miles onto the loop, and change this ride to a three-wheeler. Call to find out about

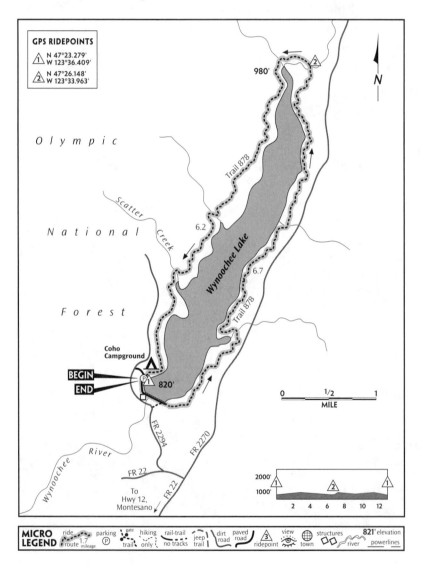

GPS RIDEPOINTS
1 N 47°23.279'
   W 123°36.409'
2 N 47°26.148'
   W 123°33.963'

980'

N

O l y m p i c

Scatter Creek

Trail 878

N a t i o n a l

6.2

Wynoochee Lake

6.7

Trail 878

F o r e s t

Coho Campground

BEGIN
END

820'

0   1/2   1
MILE

FR 2294

FR 2270

Wynoochee River

FR 22

FR 22

To
Hwy 12,
Montesano

2000'
1000'
1   2   1
2   4   6   8   10   12

MICRO
LEGEND   ride route 1.7 mileage   parking P   gate   hiking trail   rail-trail only   jeep no tracks trail   dirt road   paved road   3 ridepoint   view   structures   town   river   821' elevation   powerlines

the current state of affairs. Until the new bridge is built, plan on a knee-deep—if not waist-deep—ford. We took our shoes off so our feet wouldn't slosh around for the rest of the ride. But it was June and we quickly discovered that, with the spring runoff still flooding, the water was chest-high. We didn't want to ride six miles on wet chammies, so we took off our bike shorts and "bucked" it across the river. Now "Wynooch," the abbreviated pronunciation of this loop, has become synonymous with "take your riding shorts off to cross the river."

To Get There

From Olympia, travel west on State Route 8, which becomes US Highway 12 west of Elma. Exit US 12 at Montesano. Start your odometer at the end of the exit ramp and turn right. At 0.2 mile, turn left on Pioneer. At 1.3 miles, turn right on Wynoochee Road. At 36.5 miles, turn left toward Wynoochee Lake. At 36.7 miles, turn right onto Forest Road 2294. Drive past the dam. At 38 miles, turn right into Wynoochee Lake Dam and Picnic Area to park.

The Ride

From the picnic area parking lot on the west side of the dam, ride toward the dam. Cross the dam and continue east until the pavement ends at the Wynoochee Lake Shore Trail trailhead, **0.4** mile. The trail climbs steeply, but levels out at **0.7** mile. Cross a bridge at **1.8** miles, then ride several switchbacks down toward the lake. Cross another bridge at **2.2** miles. At **3** miles, scramble around a washout. When you reach a road, **3.2** miles, go straight. At **3.3** miles, just before the lake, bear right to reconnect with the trail.

For the next few miles, the trail is usually perfect—with a few washed-out sections—and easy to follow as it rolls around the eastern edge of the lake, past impressively big trees. At **5.8** miles, cross a dirt road and continue along the trail. At **6.1** miles, turn right onto the jeep trail and ride fifty yards to the end, where the trail resumes (if you turn left on the jeep trail and ride to the lake, you'll find an excellent picnic area). Stay on the main trail to the river, **6.6** miles.

WHOA! While the current doesn't flow particularly fast, the river can be quite deep during high water. Ford the river with care. **WHOA!** Another difficulty at this juncture involves tricky route finding—pay attention. After you've crossed the river, find the trail about 100 yards upstream to the right. From here, follow the orange flagging to the left; the trail is at times difficult to follow through a washout and over a boggy area. Soon, about **7.3** miles,

the route stabilizes and the trail switchbacks up a steep bank. Scramble across a washout at **8.3** miles. After more climbing followed by a nice descent, cross through an old stream bed.

At **9.4** miles, the trail reaches a road: Turn right. At **9.6** miles, turn left, following the "trail" signs. You'll have to walk through two more washouts. When the trail kisses a road at **11.3** miles, remain on the trail, bearing left. Reach a T at **11.7** miles: Turn right. From here, stay on the main trail, which hugs the lakeshore. Cross a road at **12.6** miles. At **12.9** miles, reach the paved parking area to complete the loop.

Option
To lessen this ride to a three-wheel rating, pedal out to the picnic area at 6.1 miles, then turn around and ride back the way you came.

Gazetteer
Nearby camping: Coho Campground
Nearest food, drink, services: Montesano

60

SOUTH OLYMPIC PENINSULA
Fall Creek
✿✿✿✿

Distance	21.6 miles
Ride	Loop; singletrack, dirt road
Duration	3 to 6 hours
Travel time	Seattle—1.5 hours; Portland—2 hours
Hill factor	Numerous climbs and descents; 980-foot gain
Skill level	Intermediate
Season	Year-round
Maps	Washington State DNR: Capitol State Forest
Users	Bicyclists, equestrians, hikers, motorized vehicles in parts
More info	Washington State DNR, Central Region, 360-748-2383

Sunny winter riding at Capitol Forest

Prelude

The trail system in Capitol State Forest is one of the best anywhere, but the trails can be muddy beyond belief, fragmented due to logging, and disorienting because there are just so many. This particular loop, on the easy side of four wheels and located primarily on the nonmotorized south side of Capitol State Forest, features several clearcuts and numerous unsigned trails, but if you hit it during dry weather and avoid the mud, you won't be disappointed. Although this loop can be ridden year-round, I'd stay away from it during wettest times of year. The last time I rode it, in the late fall but after two weeks of nice weather, the mud was bad enough that I couldn't use my small front chainring after the halfway point. Note: I have heard reports of

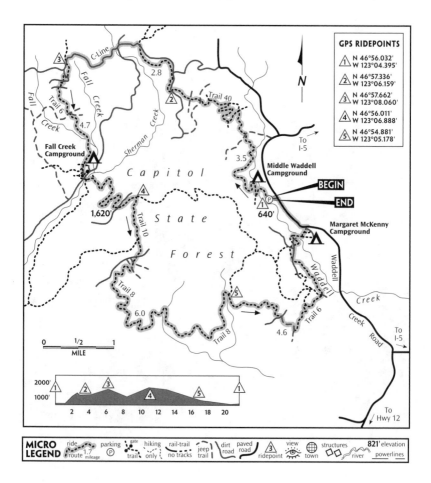

cars being broken into here, so, as at any trailhead, don't leave valuables in your car.

To Get There

Take Interstate 5 to a few miles south of Olympia and take exit 95. Zero out your odometer at the end of the exit ramp. Take State Route 121 straight through Littlerock to a T, 4 miles, and turn right onto Waddell Creek Road toward McKenny Camp. At 6.6 miles, pass McKenny Camp on the left. At 7.3 miles, turn left into the large Middle Waddell parking area.

The Ride

Follow the "trail" sign from Middle Waddell trailhead parking area. The trail winds around the back of the camp area, which is on the right, and then descends. At **0.3** mile, bear left and cross Waddell Creek. Reach a fork at **0.4** mile and turn left. After a short climb and traverse, descend to the creek again and cross it. Just past the creek crossing, take the right fork. Reach a fork at **1.3** miles and bear left. From here, the wide dirt trail noodles through the woods. At **1.6** miles, cross a dirt road. The trail begins a steady climb here. The first four and a half miles of the trail are open to motorcycles, and steep sections of the trail are rutted due to the clay consistency of the soil. After a steep climb, reach a four-way intersection at **2** miles: Go straight. At **2.2** miles, meet another four-way intersection: This time, turn left. Ignore a trail on the left at **2.3** miles, then switchback up a ferned hillside. At **2.5** miles, bear to the left and continue up. Reach another fork at **2.6** miles; again, bear left.

As you descend, ignore two trails on the right. Follow the trail across old jeep tracks at **3** miles and again at **3.3** miles. Descend to a dirt road, D-4400, at **3.5** miles. After crossing the dirt road, the trail bends to the right and parallels it. Ignore the numerous trails that spur up to the road on the right. Pass a trailhead on the right and continue along the level, winding singletrack. At **4.7** miles, reach a T at a dirt road, C-Line. Turn left and ride up C-Line, which ascends gradually. Pass a dirt road on the right and then on the left—pedal straight up the main dirt road. **WHOA!** At **6.3** miles, take an easily missed, unmarked singletrack on the left. From here, the loop traverses nonmotorized trails. The trail enters a recent clearcut. Reach a logging road, turn left, then find the trail again on the right. As you wind through the clearcut, you'll cross three more dirt roads.

Finally the trail cruises into the woods again at **7** miles. After a few quick turns, reach a dirt road, **7.4** miles. Turn right, then find the trail exiting on

the left, between a fork in the road. The trail zips down a slope, then crosses West Fork Fall Creek at **7.8** miles. Ignore three promising trails on the left, following the signs toward Mima trailhead. At **8.2** miles, ride straight through a four-way intersection of trails. Reach a fork at **8.5** miles and bear left. A few pedal strokes farther, arrive at Fall Creek trailhead. Bear to the right and take the narrow trail. The trail forks immediately—turn left. After a couple of turns, reach a dirt road and turn right. The dirt road ends at a major dirt road, D-3000. Cross D-3000 and take the singletrack, which soon crosses Sherman Creek. After the bridge, the trail forks at **8.8** miles: Turn left. When the trail forks again, bear right, away from the creek.

Immediately, you begin ascending a steep, wooded hillside. After many challenging switchbacks interspersed with long traverses, cross a dirt road, **10.8** miles, at the simultaneous midpoint and high point of the ride. The trail traverses an open slope, then drops to a T at **11** miles. Turn right onto Trail 20 toward Mima trailhead. Ride a quick, zippy trail to a fork, **11.6** miles, and turn left on Trail 8. The narrow trail gently traverses up to a road at **12.1** miles. Bear right on the road and, after three pedal strokes, pick up the trail again. After crossing two more lesser roads and traversing through an older clearcut, begin a ripping descent, switchbacking down toward Mima Creek. Cross a dirt road at **14.5** miles, then soon cross the creek. After a short climb, ride along this fun trail, crossing dirt roads at **15.7** miles and **16.1** miles.

Cross East Fork of Mima Creek, and ride a gentle uphill traverse to Mima Falls at **16.6** miles.

From the falls, continue on to a fork at **17** miles: Bear right. The trail—sometimes sweet, sometimes wide, and sometimes really, really muddy—meanders to a dirt road at **18.5** miles. Cross the road, bearing slightly right, to the singletrack on the opposite side. The trail becomes a doubletrack, then forks at **18.7** miles: Turn left on Green Line 6. Cross a road, then reach a second road and veer right. After a few yards, turn left onto the trail. At **19.1** miles, take the right fork. At a beaver pond, **19.2** miles, take a hard left turn (away from the firing range). The trail immediately forks—take the right fork of Waddell Loop.

At **20.1** miles, reach a dirt road and turn right. When the road forks at **20.2** miles, take the lesser road on the right. At **20.3** miles, turn right onto Green Line Trail 6, which wraps around a short knoll. Turn right at the fork and follow a bend around to a bridge over Waddell Creek at **20.5** miles. At **20.6** miles, take the left fork up a short but steep hill. Bear to the left again at **20.7** miles. Reach the paved entrance road to McKenny Camp at **20.8** miles and turn left. After a few chain rotations, reach Waddell Creek Road and turn left. Ride up this paved road to the Middle Waddell trailhead parking area to complete the loop, **21.6** miles.

Gazetteer

Nearby camping: Margaret McKenny Campground
Nearest food, drink, services: Littlerock

61 **Ocean Shores**

Distance	13 miles
Ride	Out & Back; sand beach; views
Duration	1 to 2 hours
Travel time	Seattle—2.5 hours; Portland—3 hours
Hill Factor	Flat
Skill level	Beginner
Season	Year-round
Maps	DeLorme: Washington Atlas & Gazetteer pages 58–59
Users	Bicyclists, hikers, vehicles
More info	Ocean City State Park, 360-289-3553

Making tracks in the sand

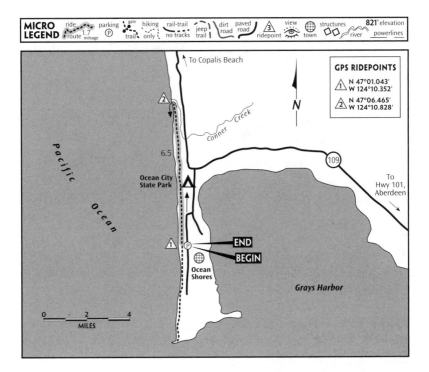

Prelude

Not much is more fun than beach riding. I never realized how confining trails and roads were until I took my bike out for a spin on the sand along the Pacific Ocean. The freedom to ride with your eyes closed is incredibly powerful. Some may tell you—emphatically—that riding on a sandy beach next to the salty ocean will put your bike on the road to the rusted scrap heap. And while it's true that salt water and sand are not the best thing for your bike, not riding it and not enjoying it are far worse. The point: Have fun with your bike; just don't ride it *into* the salt water.

To Get There

From Olympia, travel west on State Route 8, which becomes US Highway 12 west of Elma. US 12 ends at US 101 in Aberdeen; take US 101 northbound. After crossing the Hoquiam River in the town of Hoquiam, turn left on SR 109, following the signs toward ocean beaches. Start your odometer here. At 17 miles, turn left on SR 115 toward Ocean Shores. At 19.7 miles, as the

Sea level

highway bears left toward the center of town, bear right and drive to the beach at 20.2 miles. Park anywhere above the high-tide line.

The Ride

From your beach parking near Ocean Shores, ride north on the beach. Ride on the hard-packed sand for better traction. **WHOA!** Pay attention to the wind: It's easy to ride downwind, but riding into the wind on the beach can be difficult. After pedaling **3.8** miles, pass Ocean City on the right. Continue north. At **6.5** miles, reach the mouth of Conner Creek. Turn around here and ride back to Ocean Shores, **13** miles.

Gazetteer

Nearby camping: Ocean City State Park
Nearest food, drink, services: Ocean Shores

Be Responsible for Yourself

The author and publisher of *Mountain Bike! Southwest Washington* disclaim and are in no way responsible or liable for the consequences of using this guide.

1. *Mountain biking is dangerous.* Cyclists can get lost, become injured, or suffer from serious fatigue. The difficulty of the trails described in this guide and the level of skill and experience required to ride safely on the trails are subjective. It is incumbent on each rider to assess his or her preparedness for a trail in light of his or her own skills, experience, fitness, and equipment.

2. *Trail conditions change without notice.* The information contained in this book, as of the date of publication, is as accurate as possible. But conditions on these routes change quickly: Storms, logging activities, stream revisions, landslides, trail construction, and development, among other things, drastically alter trails, in some cases making them dangerous or unridable.

3. *Do not ride on private property.* Some of the rides described in this guide traverse onto private land. Do not conclude that the owner has granted you permission to use the trails listed in this book. Some landowners post signs that allow nonintrusive, daytime use by bicyclists and other users. If the property is not signed, and you are not sure of its status, obtain permission from the owner before riding on the property.

4. *Public jurisdictions may change rules at any time.* Most of the rides described in this guide are located on public land. Although these are currently legal rides, in the future land managers may decide to exclude bicycles, regulate bicycle use, or require permits. Understanding the laws as they change is up to you.

The author and publisher assume absolutely no responsibility for these or any other problems that may occur, nor should they. Hey kids, be responsible for yourselves and the land you are using.